DATE DUE			

IN THE SAME SERIES

Donald Barthelme   *M. Couturier and R. Durand*
Saul Bellow   *Malcolm Bradbury*
Richard Brautigan   *Marc Chénetier*
John Fowles   *Peter Conradi*
Seamus Heaney   *Blake Morrison*
Philip Larkin   *Andrew Motion*
Doris Lessing   *Lorna Sage*
Joe Orton   *C. W. E. Bigsby*
Thomas Pynchon   *Tony Tanner*
Philip Roth   *Hermione Lee*
Kurt Vonnegut   *Jerome Klinkowitz*

HAROLD
PINTER

GUIDO ALMANSI
and
SIMON HENDERSON

METHUEN
LONDON AND NEW YORK

First published in 1983 by
Methuen & Co. Ltd
11 New Fetter Lane, London EC4P 4EE
Published in the USA by
Methuen & Co.
in association with Methuen, Inc.
733 Third Avenue, New York, NY 10017

Typeset by Rowland Phototypesetting Ltd
Printed in Great Britain by
Richard Clay (The Chaucer Press) Ltd
Bungay, Suffolk

British Library Cataloguing in Publication Data

Almansi, Guido
Harold Pinter.—(Contemporary writers)
1. Pinter, Harold—Criticism and interpretation
I. Title   II. Henderson, Simon   III. Series
822'.914   PR6066.I53Z/
ISBN 0-416-31710-3

Library of Congress Cataloging in Publication Data

Almansi, Guido, 1931–
Harold Pinter.
(Contemporary writers)
Bibliography: p.
1. Pinter, Harold, 1930–   —Criticism and
interpretation.   I. Henderson, Simon.   II. Title.
III. Series.
PR6066.I53Z592   1983   822'.914   82-22902
ISBN 0-416-31710-3 (pbk.)

CONTENTS

General editors' preface 6
A note on the texts 9
Biographical note 10
1 Introduction 11
2 Games 24
3 Questioning games: the early plays 34
4 Hiding games: *The Caretaker* 49
5 Critical games: *The Homecoming* 59
6 Endgames: a period of transition 74
7 Memory games: *Old Times*, *No Man's Land* and
Betrayal 83
8 Different ball games: *The French Lieutenant's
Woman* and *Other Places* 95
Notes 102
Bibliography 108

GENERAL EDITORS' PREFACE

Over the past twenty years or so, it has become clear that a decisive change has taken place in the spirit and character of contemporary writing. There now exists around us, in fiction, drama and poetry, a major achievement which belongs to our experience, our doubts and uncertainties, our ways of perceiving – an achievement stylistically radical and novel, and likely to be regarded as quite as exciting, important and innovative as that of any previous period. This is a consciousness and a confidence that has grown very slowly. In the 1950s it seemed that, somewhere amidst the dark realities of the Second World War, the great modernist impulse of the early years of this century had exhausted itself, and that the post-war arts would be arts of recessiveness, pale imitation, relative sterility. Some, indeed, doubted the ability of literature to survive the experiences of holocaust. A few major figures seemed to exist, but not a style or a direction. By the 1960s the confidence was greater, the sense of an avant-garde returned, the talents multiplied, and there was a growing hunger to define the appropriate styles, tendencies and forms of a new time. And by the 1970s it was not hard to see that we were now surrounded by a remarkable, plural, innovative generation, indeed several layers of generations, whose works represented a radical inquiry into contemporary forms and required us to read and understand – or, often, to read and *not* understand – in quite new ways. Today, as the 1980s start, that cumulative post-war achievement has acquired a degree of coherence that allows for critical response and understanding; hence the present series.

We thus start it in the conviction that the age of Beckett, Borges, Nabokov, Bellow, Pynchon, Robbe-Grillet, Golding, Murdoch, Fowles, Grass, Handke and Calvino, of Albee, Mamet, Shepard, Ionesco, Orton, Pinter and Stoppard, of Ginsberg, Lowell, Ashbery, Paz, Larkin and Hughes, and many another, is indeed an outstanding age of international creation, striking experiment, and some degree of aesthetic coherence. It is a time that has been described as 'post-modern', in the sense that it is an era consequent to modernism yet different from it, having its own distinctive preoccupations and stylistic choices. That term has its limitations, because it is apt to generate too precise definitions of the contemporary experiment, and has acquired rather too specific associations with contemporary American writing; but it does help concentrate our sense of living in a distinctive period. With the new writing has come a new criticism or rather a new critical theorem, its thrust being 'structuralist' or 'deconstructive' – a theorem that not only coexists with but has affected that writing (to the point where many of the best theorists write fictions, the best fictionalists write criticism). Again, its theory can be hermetic and enclosing, if not profoundly apocalyptic; but it points to the presence in our time of a new sense of the status of word and text, author and reader, which shapes and structures the making of modern form.

The aim of 'Contemporary Writers' is to consider some of the most important figures in this scene, looking from the standpoint of and at the achievement of the writers themselves. Its aims are eclectic, and it will follow no tight definition of the contemporary; it will function on the assumption that contemporary writing is by its nature multidirectional and elusive, since styles and directions keep constantly changing in writers who, unlike the writers of the past, are continuous, incomplete, not dead (though several of these studies will address the careers of those who, though dead, remain our contemporaries, as many of those who continue to write are manifestly not). A fair criticism of living writers must be assertive but also

7

provisional, just as a fair sense of contemporary style must be open to that most crucial of contemporary awarenesses, that of the suddenness of change. We do not assume, then, that there is one right path to contemporary experiment, nor that a self-conscious reflexiveness, a deconstructive strategy, an art of performance or a metafictional mode is the only one of current importance. As Iris Murdoch said, 'a strong agile realism which is of course not photographic naturalism' – associated perhaps especially with British writing, but also with Latin-American and American – is also a major component of modern style.

So in this series we wish to identify major writers, some of whom are avant-garde, others who are familiar, even popular, but all of whom are in some serious sense contemporary and in some contemporary sense serious. The aim is to offer brief, lucid studies of their work which draw on modern theoretical issues but respond, as much modern criticism does not, to their distinctiveness and individual interest. We have looked for contributors who are engaged with their subjects – some of them being significant practising authors themselves, writing out of creative experience, others of whom are critics whose interest is personal as well as theoretical. Each volume will provide a thorough account of the author's work so far, a solid bibliography, a personal judgement – and, we hope, an en-larged understanding of writers who are important, not only because of the individual force of their work, but because they are ours in ways no past writer could really be.

Norwich, England   MALCOLM BRADBURY
                                                      CHRISTOPHER BIGSBY

A NOTE ON THE TEXTS

Quotations from Harold Pinter's works are taken from the four-volume Eyre Methuen 'Master Playwrights' edition (listed in the Bibliography), published with the same pagination by Grove Press in New York. Roman numerals refer to the particular volume, arabic to the particular page (e.g. IV, 13 indicates Volume 4, p. 13). *The Hothouse*, which is not included in the 'Master Playwrights' volumes, has been published as a Methuen Modern Play (London: Eyre Methuen, 1980), and page numbers refer to that edition. References to Pinter's screenplay of *The French Lieutenant's Woman* are to the edition published by Jonathan Cape in association with Eyre Methuen (London, 1981).

Since Pinter makes frequent use of the ellipsis for dramatic effect, we have used square brackets [. . .] in quotations from plays, to indicate where words have been omitted by us.

BIOGRAPHICAL NOTE

Harold Pinter was born in 1930 in Hackney, a deprived part of the East End of London. The only child of Jewish parents, he was educated at Hackney Downs Grammar School and brought up in the violent streets of the working-class districts of London. At 18, he joined the Royal Academy of Dramatic Art, only to feign a nervous breakdown to begin a nine-year career as a repertory actor (1949–57). During this time, he met Vivien Merchant, his first wife, by whom he had a son (Daniel). He also underwent two trials, risking imprisonment, as a conscientious objector to National Service. In 1957 *The Room* appeared at a request from a university acquaintance. This was followed in 1958 by *The Birthday Party* (which had a disastrous one-week run in London) and then, more successfully, by *The Caretaker* in 1960 which established Pinter's name both at home and abroad. Over the last twenty-five years, a string of successes in the West End and on Broadway have established his reputation as perhaps Britain's premier dramatist as a writer of stage and radio plays, television and film scripts. He has also worked as a director of both his own plays and those of others (Simon Gray in particular). In 1980 his marriage with Vivien Merchant was dissolved and he married Lady Antonia Fraser, a writer. Miss Merchant, a commanding actress in her own right, died in 1982.

1

INTRODUCTION

Like many of his contemporaries on the continent, Harold Pinter is a writer who refuses to broadcast a message to the world. He is an author without authority, a communicator in the paradoxical position of having nothing to say. He is our contemporary in a sense that many of his fellow writers in Britain – and the British theatre, in particular – are not. For him, as for the post-modernist world generally, it is *language* that provides the supreme obstacle. He is not part of that fatal tradition in English literature, going back to G. B. Shaw and the theatre of ideas, to D. H. Lawrence and the literature of feelings, according to which language is no problem – the supposed problems being intellection (the manipulation of ideas) and sincerity (the expression of feelings). 'Language is words. . . . It's bridges, so that you can get safely from one place to another': this is the claim in the first act of Arnold Wesker's *Roots*; and the belief in the conductive power of words – a belief somewhat remote from the main currents of modern European literary practice – permeates a great deal of contemporary English drama (not only the works of Wesker, but those of Osborne and Arden, of Mercer and Mortimer, of Bond and Shaffer). At the core of their shared belief lies an immoderate faith in a language of enlightenment, whereby words are used mimetically to throw light on the most obscure areas of life (as if Wittgenstein's *Philosophical Investigations* had been in vain, or had never superseded the *Tractatus*). Pinter, however, is aware that 'The more acute the experience

11

the less articulate [is] its expression' (I, 11). He is concerned with manipulating not a language of enlightenment but a language of obfuscation; not a language of social progress but a language of existential survival; not a language of communal faith but a language of divisive strategy. The words of his plays are intransigent and intransitive: they cannot be transferred to other levels of meaning, be they philosophical, ideological or allegorical. You can play all sorts of critical games with them, but it is a mistake, as we shall show, to consider them out of the context of their dramatic precincts. In Pinter words are not bridges: they are barbs to protect the wired enclosure of the self.

If we were to trace with the firm hand of a surveyor or an accountant the graph of Harold Pinter's progress, or regress, or dramatic itinerary, from the earliest works to the latest plays, a few trends would emerge: a progressive baring of the symbolic superstructure; new disguises of a violence that turns purely verbal or goes underground; monologues spreading, following perhaps some Beckettian suggestions; intensification of pauses and silences, which become the natural repositories of meaning. But the fundamental element, language, has hardly changed. From *The Room* (written in 1957) to *Other Places* (performed in 1982), Pinter has systematically forced his characters to use a perverse, deviant language specialized in concealing reality. He has remained in this respect a great ironist (again following the continental fashion: 'ironic' in the Romantic sense described by Heine and Kierkegaard, for whom God and Shakespeare were respectively the supreme ironists; not in the modern acceptation). Whatever Pinter says is never to be taken entirely seriously; for irony – that radical doubt about the very words that he uses to communicate – invariably accompanies his every statement. To miss the irony in the text is equivalent to missing the text itself. Irony creates the distance between 'Puzzling Pinter'[1] and ourselves, and demarcates a fine zone between the author and his characters, or between each of the mutually non-comprehending characters themselves. Being an honest writer, Pinter can only warn us that the material he is selling us (words) is made up of coins that

12

ring false. Hence he is unreliable and conscientious about advertising his unreliability; honest in revealing his dishonesty. In twenty years of playwriting he has never stooped to use the degraded and ultimately treacherous language of honesty, sincerity or innocence, which has contaminated the British theatre for so long.

Pinter, unlike so many other playwrights, did not have to wait for his own technical maturity as a dramatist before he acquired the language of deceit and meretriciousness (as so often happens with writers who reach a strategic idiom only after a first juvenile production of freewheeling expression-ism). His language was never chaste, but corrupt from birth. In his plays, even the virginal page protected by its candour is polluted, for the blanks convey a substructure of evil intentions and vile meanings. Pinter's idiom is essentially human because it is an idiom of lies and stratagems.[2] He has never comprom-ised with the audience that comes to the theatre to be com-forted, entertained, consoled, patronized, instructed, preached at and enlightened. He has only whispered dark words of warning (which makes his international success the more remarkable). He has always used words as incantations with-out letting us know to which religion his rituals belong.

*

Let us suppose, for a moment, that we intend to *understand* the playwright. There ought to be at least three basic avenues leading to the inner core of the works of a contemporary dramatist like Pinter: through the theatrical tradition, through the author's ideas or through character analysis. The first two are familiar enough from most contemporary critical writing, and the third is the faithful carthorse, a popular starting-point through the ages. Technique, ideas (or ideology, or philos-ophy), psychology: these are the three plausible approaches, helping us towards a better *understanding* of the modern dramatic text. One may have faith in the playwright's dramatic technique, and seek to connect his works with some modern theatrical movement (such as the Theatre of the Absurd); or

13

one may rely on the clarity and soundness of his ideas, and eventually relate them to an ideological stance or philosophical mode of thinking (such as existentialism); or one may treat the plays psychologically, and depend on what the characters say, wish to say, ought to say or do not say, trusting the author's power to breathe life into his dramatis personae and create characters who are consonant with his own ideas.

Ordinarily, each of these approaches might seem eminently sensible. Yet, though recognizing the considerable achievements of these critical methods, we do not feel any special attraction towards them. We are not sure about their adequacy for any dramatist, but we are quite convinced that they are either unsuited or inadequate, as far as a study of Harold Pinter is concerned. We are starting this essay from a position of radical doubt about Pinter's innovatory technique in the theatre (he is actually, in our view, a very traditional dramatist); of great caution and even suspicion when faced with the intimation of a 'Pinteresque' idea (about the way his ideas are meant to percolate to the various layers of speech, infiltrating the dialogue of his plays; or about the connection between the 'ideas' of the plays and the 'ideology' of the author); of total mistrust with regard to the reliability of his characters and to the existence of an umbilical cord connecting playwright and characters. For us, and apparently also for Pinter, these avenues appear to lead nowhere, ending in a cul-de-sac, a closed-system circuitry like the Bolsover Street maze (where you can only enter but never get out), so graphically described in *No Man's Land* (iv, 120).

The first avenue, the traditional cul-de-sac of compulsory *avant-gardisme*, presumes that, since modernism has been such a great leap forward over the barrier of naturalism, all successive movements should follow the same athletic model, thrusting themselves over more and more hurdles in order to keep abreast of each innovation. Now we are not denying that the moral and intellectual claims of *avant-gardisme* and stylistic progress (in spite of the pitfalls of the latter term) have certainly benefited vast areas of the contemporary theatrical scene; but with Pinter there is nothing particularly exciting to learn in

14

terms of dramatic innovations or scenic experiments, as the author himself is more than willing to admit.[3] His plays are conceived for an orthodox proscenium stage; they are conventionally based on speech and dialogue with only a marginal inference of physical action; they are written fully and intensely, their author seeming to abhor improvisation, 'happenings', or any kind of aleatory technique[4] (in this sense Pinter is definitely not a post-modernist playwright). They are set, moreover, in well-defined social milieux, scrupulously avoiding all surrealistic temptations. Above all, they belong quite clearly to a line of perversely well-made plays. (Isn't it perverse to write a play *à la* Beckett as well made as a boulevard vaudeville or a Noel Coward farce? Yet this is what Pinter does.) What is new in Pinter lies not within the area of his dramatic technique; excellent though this is, it is hardly avant-garde.

The second cul-de-sac is the critic's habitual search for a meaning and a message: the two bonuses that both critics and spectators expect at the end of a theatrical experience. There are writers who have climbed the platform of fame with a locked attaché case, secure in their knowledge that some critic will discover the number to open the ciphered lock and reveal the symbolic system of their works. With Pinter, however, as we have already suggested, no matter how fiercely you assault his plays, how thoroughly you shake out their dust with a carpet-beater, hoping to catch the fluttering mote of a meaning, the speck of dirt of a message, you get nothing except the few truisms we all knew before we started. Of course, we emerge from a Pinter play (after watching it or reading it or 'inspecting' it for critical analysis) with a firmer conviction that communication between human beings is difficult and often dangerous; that family ties are loose and often harmful; that social connections are untrustworthy and often deadly; that memory is unreliable and often treacherous; that others are always a mystery to us as we are to them (and as we are even to ourselves); that man is alone in this miserable world. Is that all? Is it worth reading Pinter if we know this beforehand? Critics who are satisfied with this lamentable booty after their message-hunting expeditions are no better than the traditional *Macbeth* reader who, in the words of Charles Marowitz, thinks that some of the greatest lines of poetry in the English language have been written in order to prove the mind-shattering truth that crime does not pay.[5] No, the greatest treasure-trove in Pinter's plays is not to be found by rummaging among his ideas: the gold lies at the end of a different rainbow. To put it in the words of Teddy in *The Homecoming*: 'It's nothing to do with the question of intelligence. It's a way of being able to look at the world. It's a question of how far you can operate on things and not in things' (III, 77). Teddy is being phoney, of course; but this does not alter the fact that, in this particular case, he can teach us a lesson.

The third cul-de-sac is the search for motivations, for psychological or psychoanalytic causes, for some kind of intellectual or emotional rationale that could help us explain why these strange beings, the Pinterian heroes, behave as they do (a *normal* key for their *abnormal* behaviour). His characters, however, are most reluctant to submit to the clumsy probing of the critical explorers with their rough surgical instruments. Faced with a Pinter play, critics become disappointed speleologists who find out that there is no hole down which they can lower themselves to discover the mysteries of psychic abysses. In fact the basic premiss of their search is missing. Psychological criticism must always start from a tacit assumption: that the character has an autonomous existence, in either an emotional or an intellectual dimension. This character, conceived by the author as an entity, is filled by osmosis with the complex network of ideas and sensations of his author and is then transferred on to that ideal stage where Hamlet and Peter Pan, Helen of Troy and Humpty Dumpty, Oedipus and Charlie Brown, are all supposed to express the full life of their roles. It is self-knowledge that makes this possible. Within *Hamlet*, Hamlet knows who Hamlet is and what Hamlet is: that is, what tremendous afterthoughts or lurid underthoughts lurk behind the awesome thoughts that he utters. The premiss is that at either a conscious or an unconscious level the author knows who his character is, and that this character himself, though fictitious, knows what he is; but the stage can offer only a token of his emotions, a sample of his ideas, a glimpse of his desires, a partial view of his complex psyche. The critic is thus the motive-monger who tries to join the dots and complete the picture, filling the gaps in the overall view, adding motivations to the character's actions, causes to his emotions, pretexts to his whims, reasons to his ideas, fuel to his passions. The critic acts as the author's humble accountant, striving to make sure that the columns of debit and credit are duly filled so that by the end of the play they will neatly match, satisfying the most severe of the playwright's moral and intellectual auditors. In our view this mopping-up operation never seems to work, either with the most uncomplicated and stereotyped characters, or with those bundles of contradictions that crowd the plays of the great masters (from Shakespeare onwards). It doesn't work with Ibsen, though at times this method might be suited to some minor Ibsenesque author such as George Bernard Shaw. Surely it is doomed to fail with the characters in Pinter's plays, who remain haunted by an uncertain identity, endowed with an ever-shifting memory, burdened with a past that behaves like a movable feast.

There is something particularly obtuse in motive-mongering about Pinter's characters, whose surface behaviour seems so often severed from the holy shrine of their inner being. They are superficial and unfathomable in their superficiality (to paraphrase Karl Kraus).[6] It is futile to analyse these characters as if they had emerged, fully armed, from the brain of Harold Pinter like Athena from the head of Zeus. Bertrand Russell imagined our world as if it had been created one minute ago with a built-in memory of a distant past in all its inhabitants. The psychological critic pursues, though unironically, a similar view, as if the playwright, by typing the letters M–I–C–K on his typewriter, had endowed Mick with a full curriculum vitae. A genuine Pinterian character, however, would not be satisfied with just one c.v.: he would need two or three. Or, better still, none, if he could get away with it. Constitutionally, he aspires to be a *voyageur sans bagages*, a disturbing passenger of the present tense, travelling light, forgoing the roughage of memory and the ballast of unfulfilled desires. But he never succeeds.

Dispensing with this sort of soul-searching is, nevertheless, partly utopian. Unfortunately we, the spectators, remain *intelligent* to a degree – intelligent in the etymological sense of choosing, collating – collecting together scraps of information, making ligaments between the inside and the outside, the literal and the metaphorical, the authorial voice and the spectatorial ear, the primary significance and the secondary suggestion. We are all kleptomaniacs, unable to leave the theatre without having first removed an ashtray and/or a message. It remains very difficult to dis-empathize, to dissociate from a character completely, shunning any pretence of ever understanding his predicament. To paraphrase Oscar Wilde: we are aware that an ethical sympathy in a spectator is an unpardonable mannerism,[7] but we cannot be asked to ignore the endemic diseases of Pinter's country: loneliness and despair; or the chronic ailments of specific characters, such as Stanley's cowardice in *The Birthday Party*, Davies's insecurity in *The Caretaker*, Max's sentimental deprivation in *The Homecoming*, Hirst's death-wish in *No Man's Land*. Yet we must control ourselves, check our sympathies, silence our inquisitive hearts. Above all, we must not pretend to dig deep. If we satisfy ourselves with what happens there and then, forgoing the time element that exists outside the text, then we will come to appreciate the role that strategy – rather than psychology – plays in these characters' behaviour. And even more so in their respective opponents: Goldberg, Mick, Lenny, Spooner. For us, Pinter criticism has a better contribution to make – through our understanding of the strategic purpose of dialogue rather than through our involvement with the characters' emotional needs. We are not being dogmatic, nor are we issuing a critical manifesto of anti-psychologism. We are simply indicating the general direction that our inquiry is going to take.

*

The death of the author in post-modernist times[8] has given rise to a corresponding birth of the reader. It is significant, then, that *The Birthday Party* – despite its initial failure – should, over the years, have become a commercial success, for this is a play which, more than any other on an English stage, heralded the triumphant emergence – or perhaps renaissance – of the reader-*participant* who contributes to the meaning of the text, and the belated exit of the passive reader, the reader-*consumer*. Pinter's plays, once labelled 'comedies of menace', are chiefly comedies of elusion, avoidance, withdrawal, mendacity and guile. Because his language is a language of escapist manœuvring, which studiously avoids the commitment of a conflict or confrontation, it requires a specialized kind of reading, one that is alert to the mercurial wriggles of the protagonists. The audience must be on the lookout for the unexpected twist, the shameless contradiction, the dazzling non sequitur, which are smuggled into the territory of a slow and apparently dull conversation. Nothing is duller *per se* than a piece of Pinterian conversation: as in Chekhov, the excitement lies in the mental speculation it provokes, not in the dull text itself. It is like conceptual art, where the focus lies on our reaction to the object, not on the object itself. Both Pinter's plays and Pinter's characters boast the fact that they can never be trusted; it is thus fatal to approach them with an open mind, a curious eye, a naïve heart. The conventional reader's honesty and integrity can be a handicap when dealing with a master of deception such as Pinter, who must be beaten at his own game. We must fight obscurity with obscurity, deception with deception, guile with guile.

One clue to reading the text is to recognize that all the plays are apparently given over to the singleminded preoccupations of *strategy*. The Pinterian hero, especially in the early plays, is often as inarticulate as a pig, stumbling pathetically over every second word, covering a pitifully narrow area of meaning with his utterances, blathering through his life. Yet he does not seem to whine or grunt or giggle or grumble to give an outlet to his instincts, desires, passions or fears. He grunts in order to hide something else. Even when he grunts (like Davies in *The Caretaker*: 'Oh, I see. Well, that's handy. Well, that's . . . I tell you what, I might do that'; II, 25), his grunt is a strategic move, or a lie. In order to contribute to these studies in obfuscation, the characters must lie. They are often abject, stupid, vile, aggressive; but they are capable enough as conscientious and persistent liars, whether lying to others or to themselves, to hide the truth, or because they no longer know truth's truthful abode. There are some who are not very good at lying, those who are incapable of planning clever strategies, and to get at *them* you must plunge the vertiginous depths of stupidity, where, for instance, Meg, the heroine of *The Birthday Party*, suffers her bovine grief. This is to descend into the abyss of idiotic speech – a dangerous exercise, as noted by one of Pinter's unrecognized masters, Heidegger. The realization dawns that the plays are often founded on an apparent contradiction: the worse the speech, the better the text – see, for instance, the dialogue in *The Dumb Waiter*, the meandering babble of two morons.

On the traditional stage, characters often use dialogue for their underhand strategy but reveal their true selves in monologues. This is not true of Pinter's plays, where both dialogue and monologue follow a technique of deviance. You can trust his characters neither when they are talking to others nor when they are talking to themselves: this is what makes *Landscape*, *Old Times* and *No Man's Land* such difficult plays. Characters shift position crab-like, move forward like knights on a chessboard – an oblique, tentative step rather than a bold progress.[9] This requires a picklock language, used askew, whose crooked insinuation – divorcing the reality of the *thing* from the reality of the *word*[10] – mocks the straight approach of the honest key.

With Pinter, expression is no longer the faithful reflection of an emotion nor the *word* of a *thing*: the mirror is slanted, and the expression therefore does not reflect the emotion that stands in front but an adjacent one, so that each sound and image is systematically distorted. The stage – and the post-Shavian English stage in particular – was used to a direct language, reflecting the inner world of mind and heart with symmetrical inevitability. Pinter replaced the right angle by an obtuse angle, so that repartees do not rebound directly: this is his trademark, his special effect which gives the odd ring to his conversations (it is a Chekhovian influence, but also possibly a borrowing from Strindberg who 'avoided the mathematically symmetrical construction of French dialogue and let people's brains work irregularly, as they do in actual life').[11]

Pinter is a crooked playwright who therefore requires a crooked, oblique reading. Rabelais imagined the reader coming to grips with his text rather in the manner of a dog coming to grips with a bone: biting it, breaking it, licking and sucking it in order to get to its 'substantive marrow'.[12] But a hard bone cannot be broken into with a frontal and perpendicular bite: it requires an oblique approach, with the back teeth penetrating in between the splinters of the bone so that the tongue can stealthily approach its succulent centre (how exciting to use the adjective 'succulent' after Pinter has transformed it into a lewd word in *The Birthday Party*, I, 27). Likewise, the reader must be cunning, aiming to penetrate diagonally in the cleft between expression and emotion, in the fissure between what is uttered and what is meant.

We hope, in this study, to offer justifications for the dishonest obliqueness of our approach. We do not pretend to crack any linguistic or psychological or symbolic or allegorical or anthropological or psychoanalytic code, for the very good reason that we do not believe any such general code exists (and, if it were to exist, it ought not to be broken, the penalty being the destruction of the text). We are inviting the readers to fight with an antagonistic text which refuses to take a collaborative stance with anyone: hence we are urging them to a battle that can only be lost (like Jacob fighting with the angel). Pinter's plays are powerfully persuasive, provided that we do not ask ourselves the final question: what (truisms apart) is it that we hope to be persuaded of? In this respect Pinter's plays are post-modernist texts, rejecting all conciliatory blandishments of an audience, all friendly gestures towards readers ever so willing to suspend their disbelief. The plays are meant to create bafflement, irritation, fear, a general sense of impotence, feelings of helplessness, a seething resentment, an acrid hostility. His are great plays one wants to hate (not unlike the scabrous masterpieces of other craftsmen of despair, from Strindberg to

Pirandello, from Wedekind to Beckett). The Romantic text went out of its way to seduce the passionate reader into sharing the exhilarating experience of its heroes; the post-Romantic writer, and Pinter in particular, requires brave spectators who are ready to face the vacuum of their own intelligence, the failure of their own perspicacity, the brutality of their own emotions. Pinter's world is tough on both sides of the limelight, and the often criticized giggle of a bemused audience during the performance of his plays acts as a simple defence mechanism, a Freudian resistance not so much against the text as against their reaction to the text. (Pinter has described the embarrassed titters of his audience as 'a mode of precaution, a smoke-screen, a refusal to accept what is happening as recogniz-able'.[13])

In Pinter, mastery over a language becomes a form of control over one's own precipitous exits, hasty withdrawals, instant disguises ('Who, me?'). If you speak fast and eloquently, you may be able to avoid taking issue and shun confrontation. In other words, language becomes the most sophisticated means of non-communication. Language, in any case, is a useful method of avoiding silence with its dreadful prospect of being left face to face with oneself. On silence we have to be silent, as Wittgenstein suggested in the final pages of the *Tractatus*, but we can use language to analyse the Pinterian language, which both on a social and on a psychic level becomes the tactical instrument of one's own cowardice, a camouflage behind which we hide not necessarily what we are, but what we fear or suspect we might be. This positive defence of language as evasion is firmly stated in the most celebrated declaration by Pinter during one of his rare interviews:

I feel . . . that instead of any inability to communicate, there is a deliberate evasion of communication. Communication itself between people is so frightening that rather than do that there is continual cross-talk, a continual talking about other things, rather than what is at the root of their relationship.[14]

The dialogue is therefore digressive, since its purpose is to misinform, or to inform your interlocutor of things he already knows according to an accepted model of idle conversation. To find such an awareness of misunderstanding and its therapeutic usage, we have to go back to Baudelaire, who preached a gospel of misconstruction. According to this view, the world owes its continuous existence to people's capacity to misunderstand each other with the full commitment of bad faith. As long as we refuse to pay attention to the voices of other people, avoid any sympathy for them, distort what we hear, everything is fine. The real enemy is understanding: the appreciation of how horrible we/you/they are (this is not very far from Freud's fear that propagating his ideas was akin to spreading the plague). Fortunately, however, mankind is saved by its congenital dishonesty. Harold Pinter has inherited part of this great lesson of cynicism, while never shying away from assuming the responsibility of tragedy and despair in his plays.

It follows that Pinter's plays can be seen as violently anti-psychological, and hence impervious to most traditional critical approaches. To search for psychological plausibility, behavioural congruity, confessional eloquence or epistemological clarification in his plays is, most of the time, a vain enterprise. Equally vain seems to us the quest for social realism, psychoanalytic symbolism, anthropological allegorism or ideological commitment – as vain as a Marxist analysis of how rich people behave in a novel by P. G. Wodehouse. Such searches and quests satisfy the critic's vanity but dull the reader's sensitivity to the text. Pinter is clearly playing a different game, one meant for poker-faced hustlers and card-sharpers, not for bingo players or crossword enthusiasts. We shall therefore attempt to be as devious as he.

23

2

GAMES

They are playing a game. They are playing at not playing a game. If I show them I see they are, I shall break the rules and they will punish me. I must play their game, of not seeing I see the game. (R. D. Laing, *Knots*)[15]

The only thing we know about Pinter's characters is that they find communication not only difficult but terrifying. As we have seen, they continually try to evade the pitfalls of human intercourse, frequently resorting to a sort of bobbing and weaving in the face of all direct contact.[16] But the time has to come when even these shy creatures must meet. Sooner or later the door will open, the room will be violated by an external presence, a confrontation must take place. At such times of emergency, alarm bells ringing, characters tend to fall back on the main resource left in their repertoire of evasive tactics: they take to playing games to keep the other at bay. But which games?

According to Roger Caillois (*Les Jeux et les hommes*, 1958), there is a radical division between the games favoured by 'primitive' societies and those favoured by 'civilized' societies (the definitions are his, not ours). The latter prefer *agon* (that is, competition; agonism; trials of strength, skill and ability; technique, training and specialization) and *alea* (chance; gambling; randomness; prediction of future events). The former prefer *ilinx* (literally, vertigo; hence, dance; dizziness; hypnosis; trance) and *mimicry* (imitation; theatrical or ritual representations; pretence or fictionality; the use of masks, disguises, etc.). These four categories, according to Caillois, cover the universe of what is playable and define the mode of behaviour of *homo ludens* in all forms of social organization.

It is no surprise to discover that Pinter's 'primitive' characters favour the games of *mimicry*, since these seem best suited to the elusiveness of their practices. Mimicry allows them to be elsewhere, to step outside their lives, to shun the responsibility of their body and image, their stance as moral individuals, their role as social beings, their location in past and present. By mimicking they become forgers who are no longer able to recognize their own artifacts from coins legitimately minted. They are as persistently unsuccessful in their counterfeiting as Walter, the artless gaol-bird in Pinter's television play *Night School* (1960). They act as monsters of psychological indeterminacy, creatures who tend to obliterate themselves by merging into the surroundings. They are amoebas – shifting beings who cannot be pinned down to a position, an opinion or an emotion. They are escaped convicts from the prison of a recognizable self, or agents parachuted into enemy territory, expecting at any moment to be caught or found out. Often they absorb their identity by osmosis from whoever is standing next to them (witness the way in which Davies becomes a caretaker in the play of the same name). In other words, they are eminently human. At times, their desperate longing not to exist seems to us one of the models of social behaviour in contemporary society.

Eric Berne, in his influential work *Games People Play*, popularized the belief that people play games to avoid the horrors of true intimacy:

> Intimacy requires stringent circumspection, and is discriminated against. . . . Society frowns upon candidness, except in privacy; good sense knows that it can always be abused; and the Child fears it because of the unmasking it involves. Hence in order to [avoid] exposing themselves to the dangers of intimacy, most people compromise for games when they are available . . .[17]

Pinter's games, in line with Berne's theory, are usually played in bad faith, as a flight from reality in the Sartrean sense or as a flight from confrontation in true ethological fashion (when in doubt, the animal runs away). His characters play games of chatting with people in the street as a way out of their isolation;

games of conversation with their partners as an evasion of hostility; games of politeness on social occasions as if to smile away the barbarity of their lives; games of concern for the wellbeing of others as if to avoid the awareness of self-seeking; games of love as a defence against hatred or indifference; games of sincerity, above all, to dispel the awful feeling that the word has no meaning whatever.

All these games are forms of *mimicry*, and they are discussed more fully in the next chapter. But there are other games in the theatre of Pinter that are played in terms of *agon* – of fight as opposed to flight – as a means of confronting reality when a clash can no longer be avoided. They then become strategic campaigns in the 'battle for positions', in the struggle for 'dominance and subservience' which Pinter admits is a repeated theme in his plays.[18] These battle games, needless to say, are fought with an uncompromising dishonesty. Behind their ritualistic aspects they purposely conceal what Berne calls the 'ulterior quality' of games, their lurking 'motivation' or underlying 'snare'.[19] Bypassing the dull phase of 'theatre of ideas' which has in many ways dominated the Western stage for the last century, Pinter's characters join forces with their ancient predecessors by becoming not carriers of thoughts but embodiments of instinctual drives; not *raisonneurs* but wily players seeking to gain the upper hand in their social interactions.

Pinter's games of *mimicry* and *agon* are both, primarily, games involving language; in Chapter 3 an attempt will be made to correlate them to, respectively, the 'phatic' and 'rhetorical' modes of communication. The notion that language itself is a kind of game is one of the major insights to be found in Wittgenstein's *Philosophical Investigations*. Communication, according to this view, is simply an exchange of various 'language games'. Like all games, these too must have rules, which are laid down in each instance, enabling the participants to communicate. Even deceit, Pinter's most typical form of communication, has to be regulated in this Wittgensteinian sense, since 'lying is a language-game that needs to be learned like any other'.[20]

The language game of chatting is, normally, a form of

extreme *dissimulation* (in which nothing is given away). There are, however, other occasions when the game of *simulation* (mendacity, false pretences, etc.) plays at least as important a role. Both games are very prominent in *The Caretaker*, where hiding and seeking are shown to be two sides of the same coin (see Chapter 4). Lying – saying the thing that is not – is, for instance, very much the name of the game in the case of Mick, the more aggressively shifty of the two brothers. All his speeches seem simulated, as if they were severed in some way from the inner core of his self. His voice does not seem to inhabit his body at all – a characteristic feat of *ostranenye*, of distancing, well brought out by the acting master of the remote voice, Alan Bates, in his classic interpretation of Mick in the London production of 1960. Jonathan Pryce played Mick in the National Theatre (London) production of 1981 as if the threats were real threats, and the flatteries simple waiting moves; Alan Bates, however, established a convention in which Mick's words appear to convey no meaning but merely intention. They have no currency outside the domain where tactical points are won or lost. In this interpretation Mick uses language as if it were a private game between two players:

> You remind me of my uncle's brother. [. . .] Had a penchant for nuts. That's what it was. Nothing else but a penchant. [. . .] Peanuts, walnuts, brazil nuts, monkey nuts, wouldn't touch a piece of fruit cake. [. . .] To be honest, I've never made out how he came to be my uncle's brother. I've often thought that maybe it was the other way round. I mean that my uncle was his brother and he was my uncle. But I never called him uncle. As a matter of fact I called him Sid. My mother called him Sid too. It was a funny business. Your spitting image he was. Married a Chinaman and went to Jamaica. (II, 40)

This is a language of total simulation that claims the right to create reality. Yet *The Caretaker* also features the alternative language of dissimulation, a game usually played out between the elder of the two brothers, Aston, and his progressively unwelcome guest, Davies, which facilitates the accustomed evasion of commitment. When their game of 'talking to each other' is mutually agreed upon, it becomes a kind of linguistic hide-and-seek:

ASTON. Well, I mean . . .
DAVIES. I mean, I'd have to . . . I'd have to . . .
ASTON. Well, I could tell you . . .
DAVIES. That's . . . that's it . . . you see . . . you get my meaning?
ASTON. When the time comes . . .
DAVIES. I mean, that's what I'm getting at, you see . . . (II, 51–2)

The strategy of this particular language game happens to be transparent in its context. Neither Davies nor Aston is prepared to make the categorical statement which might prove incriminating. They know that whatever they say might be used against them in the court of Mick's flat, so they exchange a wary 'no comment' in the form of idle talk and leave it at that. In legalistic terms, they have nothing to say, for neither will commit himself to meaning what he says, or saying what he means – in the unlikely hypothesis that they ever knew what they intended to mean in the first place. The sound of their voices signifies that they are talking, but what they are talking about is outside the domain of meaning. Pinter is here exploring that dizzy area of nonsense where words tend to return to their status as mere sounds, *flatus vocis*.

Keeping things hidden is a general rule that one breaks at one's peril in Pinter's plays. As Peter Hall, Pinter's most empathetic stage-director, puts it: 'To shout . . . is a weakness. You have to contain everything' (though to be silent is a different form of weakness).[21] Pinter and his characters play their cards very close to their chests, so the reader/spectator is never in a position to understand what is really going on. At some privileged moments he can surmise what games are being played – but even that can prove an arduous task. The reader has to delve between the lines of the text, 'where under what is said, another thing is being said' (I, 14), studying the articulacy of silences, the eloquence of latency. As with Chekhov, one has

28

to reach into the subtext of the unspoken, for rarely is there the comfort of a stated unequivocal fact. Only at times of extreme pressure, during the 'irrevocable' moments when a character has for once to 'say what he in fact means', when what he says is unprecedented and 'can never be taken back' (i, 15), is the level of discourse made clear, and then the glimpse is but fleeting, a snatched truth among lies. At such times, the game breaks down, for these are all lucid encounters which have to be played behind masks.

This is particularly true in *The Homecoming*, which we shall discuss in Chapter 5. The crisis comes here when Teddy, the success of the family who had been in voluntary exile prior to his homecoming, breaks the implicit rules of his clan by taking Lenny's cheese roll (iii, 79). By bringing the 'battle for positions' between himself and his brother into the open, by making their dispute physically present (in the form of the stolen cheese roll), he breaks the one cardinal rule that still operates in his father's household, which is to make sure that everything stays hidden. With this futile act of manifest aggression, Teddy leaves his defences wide open – a family trait displayed by his other brother, Joey, the failed boxer, who doesn't 'know how to defend' himself and doesn't 'know how to attack' (iii, 33) – and is shown to be in defiance of the Queensberry Rules of familial infighting. His civilized boxing match with Lenny becomes an all-in wrestling brawl with the 'barefaced audacity' of this illegal move, and Lenny, hit below the belt, is not slow to declare his first public warning:

> Well, Ted, I would say this is something approaching the naked truth, isn't it? It's a real cards on the table stunt. I mean, we're in the land of no holds barred now. Well, how else can you interpret it? To pinch your younger brother's specially made cheese roll when he's out doing a spot of work, that's not equivocal, it's unequivocal. (iii, 80)

Such occasions, however, are rare, since Pinter does not often declare his hand in moments of truth; the moment of mendacity can be, dramatically, as rewarding.

To break the rules deliberately, like Teddy, is to be a

'spoilsport' who, in the words of Huizinga, 'shatters the play-world itself' and 'by withdrawing from the game [attempts to rob] the play of its illusion'.[22] Sarah in *The Lover* (II, 194) and Bill in *The Collection* (II, 152) are actually described as spoil-sports; Gibbs also acts the spoilsport in *The Hothouse* when his fellow interrogator Miss Cutts throws him a ping-pong ball and says 'Catch!' (p. 118); in the text, he puts the ball in his pocket, but he crushed it underfoot in the Hampstead produc-tion of 1978, directed by the author. Stanley, the sullenly slothful lodger in *The Birthday Party*, is a would-be spoilsport who is forced to join in and consequently to lose. Immediately 'sulky' from the outset, he refuses to take part in the seductive Oedipal games of his landlady, Meg. He even tries to spoil his own 'birthday' party by first attempting to strangle Meg and then sexually assaulting Lulu, the nagging girl from next door. This gives Goldberg and McCann, the two men sent by an unspecified 'Organization', a pretext for casting him out of society and sending him back to their headquarters (*chez* 'Monty's') for 'special treatment'. One must always obey the golden rule that exists in such communities, it seems, which, in Goldberg's borrowed words, is to 'Play up, play up, and play the game' (I, 87).[23]

Whereas Stanley does all he can to spoil other people's games, there are some in Pinter who want to join in but are incapable of finding partners (like the voice delivering *Mono-logue*, who challenges a non-existent opponent to a game of ping-pong), while there are others who are unable to persuade their partners to play (like Duff who is frustrated by his wife's not returning the conversational ball in *Landscape*; or Law who is humiliated by his rival's last-minute decision not to run the race in *The Basement*). The major difficulties to arise, however, are when there are actually *too many* players. Three, in particular, seems an awkward number to play with, for couples tend to unite against the third (as in *The Caretaker*, most notably, with the two brothers uniting to evict the tramp). In many of the later plays, the appearance of a third character often sets the scene for a complex triangulation of hostile forces. In *Betrayal*, for example, Robert and Jerry play a gentle trial of strength, an urbane battle of wits for the attentions of Emma. Robert, Emma's husband, aggrieved by her clandestine adultery with the best man at their wedding, retaliates by inviting Jerry to play squash, sublimating the potential bitterness of his struggle in a game where psychological humiliation is a substitute for physical subjugation, since the metaphorical 'beating' at squash is as severe as the literal 'beating' at boxing. Cricket, of course, is the ideal Pinterian game, since it provides ample metaphorical opportunities for cross-references between sportive antagonism and social competition; but squash is also widely exploited in his plays, because here the sporting metaphors are so close to the 'real' sport. Take, for instance, the following exchange from *The Basement*:

> STOTT. The cricket. The squash courts. You were pretty hot stuff at squash, you know.
> LAW. You were unbeatable.
> STOTT. Your style was deceptive.
> LAW. It still is.
>
> > LAW *laughs*.
>
> It still is!
> STOTT. Not any longer. (III, 162)

The deception is present both in the style of playing and in the style of talking. Stott lures Law into a position of false security in the same way that Law, who had a deceptive style, would lure his opponent into making a mistake on the court. To talk in this way is a form of game, and to play is a form of battle. (Spooner combines all three levels when talking to Hirst in *No Man's Land*: 'I could advance, reserve my defences, throw on a substitute, call up the cavalry, or throw everything forward'; IV, 82.)

The game-as-battle metaphor is a recurring theme in many of Pinter's screenplays, where the hostility of a love triangle often takes the form of a violent game of sport between two men. In *The Servant*, Tony and Barrett's jostling for position *vis-à-vis* Susan (and *vis-à-vis* life) is best seen in the improvised game of 'ball' on the staircase, where the master tries to defend his position at the top of the flight of stairs – and at the top of the social ladder – against his more able opponent, his servant. Later on in the film, the positions seem about to be reversed, as Tony, the supposed master, is seen cowering at the top while his servant comes charging up the stairs to 'find him out' in a manic game of hide-and-seek (all this is played in a house in Chelsea as if it were a test to prove one's manhood in the jungle). Another game of improvised 'ball' takes place in the cloistered environs of *Accident*, as William and Stephen, teacher and pupil, compete bloodily (with 'teeth bared' at one stage) for the aristocratic Anna von Granz. The clearest case, though, of a sporting match being used to convey a hidden conflict is the game of cricket played in *The Go-Between* (all three of these films, incidentally, were directed by Joseph Losey, who seems Pinter's most congenial *film* director).[24] In this film, from L. P. Hartley's novel, Trimingham and Ted Burgess, the two competitors for Marian, are brought into direct and open confrontation on the cricket field of battle. The violence that had been simmering between them under the façade of genteel Edwardian politeness explodes with sudden ferocity in Burgess's 'savage' hitting of sixes off Trimingham's bowling. It is a *topos* that reappears in *The French Lieutenant's Woman*, Pinter's most recent film script to date, where a typical scene is inserted – not in Fowles's novel – which has Charles engaging in a 'violent, intense' game of real tennis with his lawyer (scene 149, p. 60). This externalizes the inner turmoil that he feels in the middle of his sentimental crisis, unable as he is to choose between Ernestina and Sarah Woodruff.

In many of these love triangles, there is a degree of what Berne calls the 'Let's You and Him Fight' game. This is typically a feminine ploy, Berne suggests, for it is usually the woman in the triangular relationship who 'manœuvres or challenges two men into fighting', the implication being that she will 'surrender herself to the winner'.[25] This is true of *The Homecoming*, where Ruth's kissing of Lenny is a direct challenge to Teddy, her ineffectual husband; and even more so of *The Basement*, where the woman, Jane, appears to encourage her two rivals, Stott and Law, to fight over her. The two men duly oblige in a series of athletic challenges or playful encounters which become progressively 'savage'. Stott wins the first round, not by defeating Law at the running race, but, as we mentioned before, by pretending to run and then standing still (Law is left as a fool; hence he has lost). This is followed by an improvised game of cricket, with Stott bowling marbles to Law, who uses a flute as a bat. And this in turn becomes a frantic power struggle, as Law 'brilliantly cuts' a marble into a fish tank, only to be sent crashing by a marble which hits him in the forehead. In the final conflictual image, we see them as they 'come at' each other in a sudden smash of broken milk bottles. At the end of the play, the succession of games appears to have turned the situation topsy-turvy; in the beginning Law had territory (the basement) and Stott had sex (with the girl); in the final scene Stott has territory (he is comfortably installed in the basement), but Law, though outside in the rain, has the girl. Who is the winner and who the loser?[26] (The same applies to *The Homecoming*: who is the winner here — Ruth with her new-found territory, or the male household with their proud new acquisition of a sexual object?) *The Basement* provides no answers; indeed, its circularity even suggests that the battle for positions is about to start all over again.

3

QUESTIONING GAMES:
THE EARLY PLAYS

To ask questions and demand answers is also a battle game in Pinter, where it usually takes two forms: either you ask a series of irrelevant questions, just to keep the language game going; or you ask an awkward question so that the other is unable to answer. Most of the time, both characters know all the questions and answers already, so that the question-and-answer sequence becomes merely a ritualized form of social intercourse. Tom Stoppard hints at a similar contest in the game played by the two courtiers in the first act of *Rosencrantz and Guildenstern Are Dead*, where the aim is to answer question with question, the loser being the player who makes the mistake of uttering an unequivocal statement (rhetoric, repetition, synonyms and non sequiturs being regarded as 'fouls'). With Pinter there appear to be two questioning games that are of particular importance, especially in the early plays, where there is a considerable predominance of the interrogative mood (a fact rarely acknowledged by the critics). The two games – the phatic, which tends to unite people, and the rhetorical, which aims at dividing them – appear to be diametrically opposed in intent (as will later be shown).

The first of these questioning games seeks to establish contact, and it is perhaps best described as the *phatic* mode of interrogation (borrowing the expression from the 'speech event' theory of Roman Jakobson, for whom the 'phatic' meant a way of making linguistic contact – such as 'Hello' or 'Good morning' – that was not designed to elicit or offer any information[27]). The phatic mode is a customary opening gambit in many of Pinter's early plays, where it typically involves a ritualized exchange over the breakfast table. There is a garrulous partner, usually female, who tries to communicate with a laconic friend, usually male, via an obtrusive third medium such as a newspaper or magazine. The idea for the game is said by Pinter to have originated in a real-life incident he encountered at a party. This was to become the creative inspiration not only for his first play, *The Room* (1957), which he wrote for a friend at the University of Bristol in just four days, but for subsequent plays which were also to feature this strange dramatic image. Pinter tells of how he went

> into a room which I'd never been into before, on one occasion, and saw two people in this room. It was rather an odd image: a little man cutting bread and making bacon and eggs for a very big man who was sitting at the table quite silent, reading a comic. The big man never spoke – I was there about half an hour – the little man had a lot to say and he was in the meantime cutting this bread and butter.[28]

Pinter seems to have seized on this central image of 'two people in a room', which developed into a great fascination both for himself and for his bemused but entranced audiences. In plays such as *The Room*, *The Birthday Party* (1957) and, at a different social level, *A Slight Ache* (1958), the little man becomes a garrulous woman. The meal itself is usually insignificant and meagre (a simple affair of 'toast and tea'[29] rather than the breakfast with champagne served up in the second act of *No Man's Land*), but the ritual behind it – the woman shouting through the hatch, the man hiding behind his newspaper – was to become an established comedy routine in Pinter, drawing on the popular cliché of the nagging wife and the withdrawn, downtrodden, almost imbecilic husband.

The constant references to food and the physical presence of the serving-hatch (or eponymous dumb-waiter) seem to suggest a connection with the British 'kitchen sink' school of working-class realistic drama which rose to prominence in the 1950s with plays such as those by Arnold Wesker and Alun

Owen. Probably Pinter was influenced to a degree; but he was always, from the very beginning, more realist than the realists ('plus royaliste que le roi'), a 'hyperrealist' in the sense the word has acquired in the modern art scene. A virtuoso of phono-mimesis, he knew how to exploit the stammerer: either the phonetic stammerer, or the conceptual stammerer, who piles up debris of words, stumps of phrases, truncated fragments of meaningful expression, to barricade the entrance to the nearest burrow where, in a cowardly way, he hid himself. Martin Esslin effectively sums up the novelty of Pinter's elegant and spectacular illiteracy: 'inarticulate, incoherent, tautological and nonsensical speech might be as dramatic as verbal brilliance when it could be treated simply as an element of action'.[30] Davies, in *The Caretaker*, is the expert in the art of stuttering acrobatics, interspersed with Pindaric flights of bad grammar: 'What about them shoes I come all the way here to get I heard you was giving away?' (II, 24). These are linguistic *tours de force*, as difficult and as artificial as the sketch of the master skater who pretends to be a clown who pretends not to know how to skate. The realist, who follows the conventions of truth-telling, is finally defeated by the hyperrealist, who follows more radical conventions of truth-telling. Pinter's famed 'ear' for naturalistic-sounding dialogue masks a deceptively well-contrived genius for the craft of linguistic construction. As is often pointed out, a tape recorder left running on a bus could never hope, as some people might imagine, to reproduce a 'Pinteresque' dialogue or a 'Pinteresque' play – whatever these might be (indeed, compare a typically banal conversation in a bus queue with the situation depicted by Pinter in 'Request Stop', a revue sketch written in 1959). In the same way, you could never expect to find in a large store or in a railway station such perfect representatives of depressed humanity as the coloured cleaning lady or the elderly tourist sitting on a suitcase who appear in the statues by Duane Hanson; to identify in the face of a neighbour such a representative image of mediocrity as the expression of one of the friends of Chuck Close immortalized by his paintings. Pinter, like these hyper-realist artists, searches for a banality to defy all banalities; for a mediocrity in front of which all other mediocrities are exceptional, to put it in the manner of the White Queen in *Through the Looking-Glass*.

The newspaper from the popular press, or the comic, often plays an important part in the breakfast ritual of these early plays (except in the well-to-do world of *A Slight Ache*, where Edward reads the solidly middle-class paper, the *Telegraph*, while his wife, Flora, natters on about honeysuckles and convolvuluses). The paper brings to the characters the endless round of daily gossip, with their inglorious titbits of meaningless trivia: 'Someone's just had a baby' (Meg in *The Birthday Party*; I, 21); 'A child of eight killed a cat!' (Ben in *The Dumb Waiter*; I, 131), and so on. Contemporary dramatists like Pinter seem peculiarly interested in the newspaper as a medium, perhaps because of the alienating effect that such trivia can have on its readers; but also because, as has been pointed out, the newspaper is 'one of the most effective barriers to communication devised by man'.[31] In both Beckett and Ionesco, there are scenes that are very similar to Pinter's phatic openings where a woman tries to reach out to her husband, only to be frustrated by the 'effective barrier' of his newspaper. All three seem fascinated on occasions by obituary columns, those endless rows of empty, meaningless statistics, which their characters try uncomprehendingly to come to terms with:

MR SMITH (*still looking at his paper*). There's a thing I can never understand. In the births, deaths and marriage columns of the paper, why the devil do they always give the age of the deceased persons and never tell you how old the newly-born babies are? It doesn't make sense. (Ionesco, *The Bald Prima Donna*)

WILLIE (*reads*). His Grace and Most Reverend Father in God Dr Carolus Hunter dead in tub. (Beckett, *Happy Days*)

BEN. Kaw! (*He picks up the paper.*) What about this? Listen to this! (*He refers to the paper.*) A man of eighty-seven wanted to cross the road. But there was a lot of traffic, see? He couldn't see how he was going to squeeze through. So he crawled under a lorry. [. . .] It's enough to make you want to puke, isn't it? (Pinter, *The Dumb Waiter*; I, 129–30)

Pinter's laconic males tend to hide behind their propped-up newspapers, reading out the occasional snippet, while their blabbering wives try to engage them in proper conversation, utilizing all the means of chatter that they know in a vain attempt to establish contact with their partners. In the absence of female characters, demanding males are also prone to chatter in these early plays: both Gus in *The Dumb Waiter* (1957; I, 135) and Davies in *The Caretaker* (1959; II, 31), for instance, are warned to stop 'jabbering' by their associates Ben and Aston respectively. The essence of chatting is to ask a barrage of silly questions either to which one knows the answers already, or which one phrases in such a way that answers are impossible to give (the non sequitur technique). This is well illustrated by what has been called the 'pregnant opening lines' to many of his plays.[32] A particularly fine example of this is the *incipit* to *The Birthday Party*, which opens with a characteristic Pinter gambit. Meg, the wife, asks a series of silly questions only to get a series of silly answers from her husband, Petey, in return:

MEG. Is that you, Petey?

   Pause.

   Petey, is that you?

   Pause.

   Petey?
PETEY. What?
MEG. Is that you?
PETEY. Yes, it's me.
MEG. What? [. . .] Are you back?
PETEY. Yes.

MEG. I've got your cornflakes ready. [. . .] Here's your cornflakes. [. . .] Are they nice?

PETEY. Very nice.

MEG. I thought they'd be nice. (I, 19)

The abyss of physical space is filled with the eternal silences of Pascal; the abyss of psychical space is filled with fragments of conversation like this. *The Birthday Party*, Pinter's first three-act play, is one of his very best studies in the art of chat. The story, in its bare outlines, tells of Stanley, a good-for-nothing layabout whose claims include having once been a concert pianist. He lives a vegetative life as the only lodger in a seaside guest house, and is taken for granted by the easygoing tenant, Petey, and cuddled and protected by his middle-aged landlady, Meg. Two visitors, Goldberg and McCann, arrive unexpectedly and frighten Stanley out of his lethargy, but it is not until the evening when a pseudo-birthday party is arranged in his honour that these fears are actively realized. He is first subjected to a brutal interrogation and then forced to join in a game of blind man's buff which ends with his being flattened against a wall, the two figures of Goldberg and McCann 'converg[ing] upon him' menacingly in the torchlight. When we next see Stanley in the final act, he appears to have been physically and mentally broken, and is able only to emit gurgling sounds from his throat. 'Clean-shaven' and 'dressed in a dark well cut suit and white collar' (I, 91), he is led away by the two mysterious strangers, and, even in his finest hour, Petey can offer only the most token resistance: 'Stan, don't let them tell you what to do!' (I, 96).

And that is all. The play is very ungenerous with information, but very exuberant in terms of sheer mindless talk. In the long exploration of the game of chatting in the modern theatre, from Chekhov onwards, Pinter has perhaps gone further and deeper than any of his fellow dramatists.[33] He is the maestro of the tittle-tattle of quotidian verbiage. Part of the difficulty that we encounter in reading his plays derives from our difficulty in facing up to the fact that these conversations, so depressingly banal, so heart-rendingly trivial, are at the core of daily life in every household. If a character in a play says 'Mother, give me the sun!', this utterance can be frightening because it is indicative of a deranged mind. Pinter has succeeded in transferring the frightening effect from the extravagance of madness to the banality of normality. He knows how to exploit the disgust of worn-out expressions, making us feel that only a deranged mind would dare to use them. The first hero of repulsive clichés is Goldberg in *The Birthday Party*. His complacent, self-satisfied articulation of rotting fragments from a language of null feeling and null sensibility succeeds in creating a fully fledged character, obscene because he uses language in its most common denominator. 'Culture? Don't talk to me about culture. He was an all-round man, what do you mean? He was a cosmopolitan' (I, 38). 'School? Don't talk to me about school. Top in all subjects. And for why? Because I'm telling you, I'm telling you, follow my line? Follow my mental? Learn by heart. Never write down a thing' (I, 87). Only Max, in *The Homecoming*, reminiscing about his family life, can create a similar feeling of revulsion for the utter emptiness of his speech. We laugh at chat, small talk, gabble, because their revelations would be too awesome if we took them seriously.

In *A Night Out*, a much-underrated radio play (1960; it was televised in Britain later in the same year to a staggering audience of 16 million), conversation crawls viscously from one pool of slime to the next. The story is very simple. Albert, a 'mother's boy' who is nagged and mocked by all the women in the play (the typists at the office party; a prostitute who picks him up; his ghastly demanding mother at home), finally rebels, but his gestures of revolt are in vain. At the end of the play he still remains the victim, tyrannized by his mother's 'love'. This is the psychological drama of the protagonist, which, paradoxically, is made more dramatic, more poetic, by the linguistic squalor of the dialogue. The exchanges between the old man and Albert's young friends at the coffee stall, the dialogue between the two office-girls at the party and the prostitute's small-minded preoccupations provide a magnificent display of linguistic horrors. There are bubbles of empty speech which explode with dismal, dampening effect when Albert's two workmates, Kedge and Seeley, comment on a football match:

> KEDGE. What's the good of him playing his normal game? He's a left half, he's not a left back.
> SEELEY. Yes, but he's a defensive left half, isn't he? That's why I told him to play his normal game. You don't want to worry about Connor, I said, he's a good ballplayer but he's not all that good.
> KEDGE. Oh, he's good, though.
> SEELEY. No one's denying he's good. But he's not all that good. I mean, he's not tip-top. You know what I mean?
> KEDGE. He's fast.
> SEELEY. He's fast, but he's not all that fast, is he?
> KEDGE (*doubtfully*). Well, not all that fast . . .
> SEELEY. What about Levy? Was Levy fast? (I, 210–11)

This fragment of conversation is painful in its vacuity. Empty chatting possesses an existential fullness when a comment upon the weather, or about the routine of daily life, disguises a fundamental question: 'Do you know that I exist?' or 'I do exist. What about you?' Kedge and Seeley are beyond that pale. Their conversation fulfils the ultimate structuralist dream: a language that speaks us instead of a language that is spoken by us. The language of the tribe ensnares the characters into deceptive demarcations. The difference between 'good' and 'all that good', 'fast' and 'all that fast', gives the speakers the illusion of free will and freedom of speech and choice. They believe that they are in control while they are being controlled. They are the puppets of language.

In normal life, language ranges from a full sensual enjoyment of the phonetic articulation in our mouth, the voicing process in our throat, the mechanics in our brain and nervous system, to a purely repetitious production of alien sounds and alien concepts,[34] as if the vocal apparatus were merely the loudspeaker of a cheap hi-fi system. At the one end we have the language evoked by William Gass: 'the use of a language like a lover . . . not the language of love, but the love of language, not matter but meaning, not what the tongue touches, but what it

41

forms, not lips and nipples, but nouns and verbs'.[35] On the other hand we have a language made of dead spittle. Pirandello understood the horror of using such debased language, 'spending again what is already spent', champing over and over words that have lived in the mouths of the dead: 'you will repeat the same words that have always been uttered. Do you believe that you are living? You are just chewing over the life of dead people' (*Henry IV*, Act II). Kedge's and Seeley's phonation resembles this form of necrophiliac articulation. In their mouths they masticate the dessicated saliva that was once in the mouth of an idiot who first *coined* these sentences; and the words of the idiot signify nothing. The two young men's destiny is the triumph of fatuousness: hence it is a tragic destiny. They cannot enjoy their football because they have been denied the linguistic capacity to utter their personal appreciation.[36] Pinter refuses – rightly, in our view – to give an intelligent voice to their inarticulate sounds in the old populist manner; but by *hyper-realizing* their sounds he gives them an audience.

If the empty talking of Kedge and Seeley is impressive, Meg's (in *The Birthday Party*) is quite exceptional. Her phatic game of questioning to establish contact ('Is that you, Petey? [. . .] Petey, is that you?') exemplifies Pinter's conception of speech as being, *inter alia*, 'a constant stratagem to cover [the] nakedness' of a vacuous existence (I, 15); but, because her threshold of shame is so much higher than anyone else's, she automatically qualifies as prize contender for the title of primadonna of chat. She certainly reigns the undisputed queen in Pinter, for she alone is able to reach those profound layers of stupidity which even characters like Rose in *The Room*, Gus in *The Dumb Waiter* and Davies in *The Caretaker* (themselves champions of meaningless gabble) cannot fathom. In any competition for chatting she would have to be considered the firm favourite, since the trivialities she utters seem as necessary to her as the very air that she breathes. Like Vladimir and Estragon in *Waiting for Godot*, she prattles on because she is 'incapable of keeping silent'.[37] In Pinter, as in Beckett, people keep silent in order to avoid talking, and talk in order to avoid

42

silence. Meg's conversation is the paradigm of existential chat, whereby you talk about nothing (or about the weather) in order to make sure that you exist – and that other people are aware of it. She plays her *futile* word games for the *serious* purpose of having her own existence confirmed by the sound of a reciprocal voice, by the mere sequence of a mutual exchange.

*

The phatic mode of interrogation thus involves a talkative character and a silent companion (or a partner of few words). The second questioning game also features both a domineering and a reluctant speaker, only here the second player is usually rendered mute by the hostile questioning of the first, and the questioning itself is often shared out between two or more interrogators (Goldberg and McCann, the two henchmen in *The Birthday Party*; Edward and Flora, the husband-and-wife team in *A Slight Ache*, etc.). This is the game of questioning to gain ascendancy, and it employs what might be called the *rhetorical* mode of interrogation. The rules are similar to those laid down by 'questions and commands', a game that was once very popular in the seventeenth century (it is mentioned, for instance, in Wycherley),[38] but which has since become obsolete. The aim is for one or more persons to address a series of absurd questions and commands to an opponent, the loser being the partner who is eventually most flummoxed.

Whereas the phatic mode is customarily found at the beginning of the plays, at the breakfast table, the rhetorical mode typically involves a staged climax of interrogation which is often preceded by an elaborate ritual of standing up and being made to sit down. The hostilities in fact open before the interrogation begins, as each player tries to force his opponent to sit down so that the interrogating party can assert its physical dominance and establish itself as master of the game (see, for example, the tense exchange between Stanley and his interrogators about who is going to sit down in the second act of *The Birthday Party*).

The rhetorical questioning game is perhaps best realized in

The Hothouse (1958). The Hothouse, it transpires, is a form of mental institution, run by the government but under the local, autocratic control of the big-businessman Roote. As the play begins, the organization is hit – or appears to have been hit (one can never quite tell with Pinter) – by a double scandal: the death in care of a patient (6457), and the impregnation of another (6459). Wishing to find the person(s) responsible, Roote passes the administrative buck to Gibbs, his second-in-command, who in turn passes it to the hapless Lamb, a junior employee who has been with the firm for only a year and seems in no way implicated in the crime. Gibbs, in league with the lascivious Miss Cutts, savagely interrogates Lamb and later claims to have forced a confession out of him. But the play ends violently with an apparent break-out by the inmates of the institution who, if Gibbs's testimony to his ministerial superiors is to be believed, slaughtered the entire staff – with only himself managing a fortuitous escape.

Though Pinter initially considered the play unfit for publication, its central interrogation scene was thought successful enough to be reproduced, in blander form, in the revue sketch 'Applicant' (1959). In the full-length play, Miss Cutts and Gibbs subject the sacrificial Lamb to a terrifying ordeal, trying to disorientate him with a wide variety of rhetorical questions (all of which would have been called 'foul' in the courtiers' game played by Stoppard). Their examination begins with a series of vague questions based on psychological typologies which are impossible to define: 'Would you say you were an excitable person . . . a moody person? . . . a social person?' Obviously Lamb finds these difficult to answer: 'Well, it depends what you mean by . . .' (p. 69). Having put him off his balance in this way, they proceed to ask him a quick-fire set of questions, not even stopping to wait for the answers:

CUTTS. Are you often puzzled by women?
LAMB. Women?
CUTTS. Men.
LAMB. Men? Well, I was just going to answer the question about women . . . (pp. 69–70)

There then follow questions that require a choice between a large number of alternatives: 'After your day's work, do you feel tired, edgy? . . . Fretty? . . . Irritable? . . . At a loose end? . . . Morose? . . .', etc. After a pause, Lamb replies meekly, 'Well, it's difficult to say, really –', an answer that is punished by the torture of an ear-piercing noise (p. 72). At this point, the questions become more and more absurd: 'Are you virgo intacta? . . . Have you always been virgo intacta? . . . From the word go?' (p. 73), 'What is the law of the Wolf Cub Pack?' (p. 74), and so on. As if to test the state of play, the examination is intensified with a multiple-choice question:

> GIBBS. When you were a boy scout, were you most pro-
> ficient at somersault, knots, leap frog, hopping, skipping,
> balancing, cleanliness, recitation or ball games? (p. 74)

They conclude for the time being with a second listed-alternative question ('Do women frighten you? . . . Their clothes? . . . Their shoes? . . .', etc.), bombarding Lamb with a further twenty-two alternatives, five of which are drowned out by the sound of loud orchestral noises.

As is customary in such questioning games, the overall effect of this great verbal assault is to reduce the opponent to a state of catatonia (the same effect is achieved by the verbal batter-ing of the unseen thought-controllers in Handke's *Kaspar*). The final image that we are left with in *The Hothouse* is of Lamb, 'electrodes and earphones attached', sitting quite still and 'staring, as in a catatonic trance'. What is he waiting for in his stupor? For the final and cruellest question, which is silence. The interrogation scene itself culminates with Lamb anxiously waiting for the next question, still willing to collaborate in the game; but no question comes, only silence. Stanley is similarly reduced to a gibbering wreck by the combined inquisitioning of Goldberg and McCann in *The Birthday Party*. Like Lamb, Aston in *The Caretaker* receives shock treatment in a mental institution to cure his subversive tendencies for 'talking too much' (II, 63–6). The use of electro-convulsive therapy (or ECT) in psychiatric practice clearly disturbed Pinter as much as it disturbed Ken Kesey (*One Flew Over the Cuckoo's Nest*).

Moreover, its loose application by the Soviet bloc in its treatment of 'socially unacceptables' as mental patients, which caused Stoppard to write *Every Good Boy Deserves Favour*, must have shocked Pinter. In 1974 he wrote a letter to *The Times*, demanding the release of one such dissident, Vladimir Bukovsky, a man imprisoned, in the author's words, 'effectively for criticizing the Soviet Government's use of psychiatric hospitals for political prisoners'.[39] Yet it is precisely because of the overt political nature of *The Hothouse* that Pinter was at first inclined to dismiss it; he believed that he 'was intentionally – for the only time, I think – trying to make a point, an explicit point, that these were nasty people and I disapproved of them.'[40] Like his characters, he clearly would have preferred to have kept things better hidden, more implicit, since he claims in the same interview to 'distrust ideological statements of any kind'. His obvious distaste for propaganda is only too clear in the way that he has Cutts and Gibbs succeed in gaining full control of Lamb's choice of words – of his language, hence of his mind. By asking Lamb a series of progressively silly questions, they come to dominate the dialogical situation purely through their blustering rhetoric.

*

As suggested earlier, the rhetorical and the phatic modes of interrogation appear to function with a diametrically opposed intent. The phatic mode aims to establish a contact or union between two partners (be this a communicative, social, familial or even sexual union), whereas the rhetorical mode aims to create a divide between two or more mutually hostile opponents. The game of establishing contact is often banal, instantly recognizable because ever so familiar; the game of asserting dominance, on the other hand, is usually shocking and absurd in its outlandishness.

The uneasy combination of these two games – the one perfectly ordinary on the surface, the other odd and threatening – often provides a jolting effect which has been described as 'a see-saw motion of violence and calm'.[41] This is complicated in many of Pinter's subsequent plays by having the two games

46

confused, so that they seem almost to merge. Some of the most chilling moments in Pinter's later plays occur when one of the characters mistakenly understands the rhetorical mode to be the phatic – while in contradistinction there are comic moments when one takes the phatic to be the rhetorical.

An example of this confusion is to be found in the opening words of *The Homecoming*, where Max employs the divisive rhetorical mode just when one had grown used to expecting from Pinter a phatic start of meaningless pleasantries. Instead of Meg's polite chit-chat about the weather or her cornflakes in *The Birthday Party*, or Davies's simple jabbering to Aston at the beginning of *The Caretaker* about having a good sit-down, we have Max's instant war-cry: 'What have you done with the scissors?' This is both a request for information and a rhetorical move to create tension, but it is answered by his son Lenny as if it were mere verbiage, empty phatic babbling: 'Why don't you shut up, you daft prat?' (III, 23). Another example of Pinter's playing with our expectations is the stunning opening remark in *The Lover*. Richard asks his wife: 'Is your lover coming today?' Normally, of course, this would be a devastatingly hostile question, meant to divide and not unite; but here it is asked '*amiably*' and is responded to in kind by Sarah's agreeable 'Mmnn' (II, 161). ('Mmnn' – and its variants, 'Mmmnn', 'Mmmmnnn', 'mmn-hmmn', etc. – are typical Pinterian responses: they are both a sign of non-committal, avoiding positive statements such as 'yea' or 'nay', and ruminative expressions of the truly 'pensive', self-reflective text.[42])

The more unnerving sort of confusion takes place, however, when a character wilfully alters the level of discourse, escalating it sharply from the phatic to the rhetorical. This is what happens in *The Collection*, when James, suspecting Bill of having committed adultery with his wife, asks him: 'Got any olives?' (II, 129). Usually a civil question with phatic intent, it is asked here rhetorically as a form of indirect threat (the stone of the olive becoming the bone of contention when James deposits it in his wallet). Mick also uses the guise of a polite question to make a veiled threat in the second act of *The Caretaker*, when he suspects Davies of trying to stir up trouble by creating division in his house. At first he appears to be wanting to establish a phatic contact with Davies by asking him for some advice about his slow-working brother. But, as Davies soon finds out, he flatters only to deceive:

MICK. [. . .] What would your advice be?
DAVIES. Well . . . he's a funny bloke, your brother.
MICK. What?
DAVIES. I was saying, he's . . . he's a bit of a funny bloke, your brother.

    MICK *stares at him.*

MICK. Funny? Why?
DAVIES. Well . . . he's funny . . .
MICK. What's funny about him?

    Pause.

DAVIES. Not liking work.
MICK. What's funny about that?
DAVIES. Nothing.

    Pause.

MICK. I don't call it funny.
DAVIES. Nor me. (II, 58–9)

Davis is confused (like the audience) because he cannot understand which level of discourse Mick is speaking on, phatic or rhetorical. Mick appears at one moment to be genuine, sincere, even straightforward, but the very next instant there is a metamorphosis, as a different mask is put on. He alternates freely between the two questioning games, making an abrupt volte-face at the least expected moment, thus disorientating his opponent and winning his objective.

4

HIDING GAMES: 'THE CARETAKER'

The trouble with playing games in Pinter's works is that the players tend to get hurt (like Stanley playing blind man's buff in *The Birthday Party*; or Law in *The Basement*, in the scene described at the end of Chapter 2). They also tend to get confused, like the audience, for it is not always clear which particular game is being played at any given moment. They are like gamblers who sit down to a game of bridge and suddenly discover that they have just lost a thousand dollars at canasta. Nor is it always obvious who is playing the game and for what (if any) reason.

Pinter integrates several different battle games into his plays, so as to disorientate his characters – and his audience. Pete, bemused by the strange behaviour of his friend Mark in *The Dwarfs* (the stage play, that is, not the unpublished novel), complains to Len – with the full backing of his mystified audience – 'Sometimes I think he's just playing a game. But what game?' (II, 101). Just as confused, Diana in *Tea Party* imperiously demands 'What game is this?' when she finds her normally calm, confident and precise husband, Disson, squatting at the door to her office and peeping through the keyhole (III, 127).

In an effort to counter the reigning scene of confusion, there are characters in Pinter who try to be quite adamant about what they mean. This is what Disson had attempted to do early in *Tea Party* when painstakingly explaining to his new brother-in-law, Willy, the 'sort of man' that he is: 'I don't like indulgence. I don't like self-doubt. I don't like fuzziness. I like clarity. Clear intention. Precise execution' (III, 113). He pursues the

American Dream of positive thinking, like Goldberg in *The Birthday Party*, Roote in *The Hothouse* and Edward in *A Slight Ache*. They all strive vainly for enlightenment, for fear of being left in the dark like Spooner at the end of the first act in *No Man's Land* (when the housekeeper, Foster, cruelly turns the light out on him both literally and metaphorically). Their blindness, however, remains. When Teddy, another of the great pretenders to a rational mode of thinking, claims that he 'won't be lost' in all the confusion of *The Homecoming*, there is an immediate blackout on the stage which effectively dampens his presumption (III, 78). There is even a character in the recently published *Family Voices* who is so determined to make himself clear that he transforms clarity into a monstrous threat:

> Compris? Comprende? Get me? Are you prepared to follow me down the mountain? Look at me. My name's Withers. I'm there or thereabouts. Follow? Embargo on all duff terminology. With me? Embargo on all things redundant. All areas in that connection verboten. (IV, 291)

This sounds like an Oxford philosopher disguised as a thug from the slums. The search for verbal precision, for semantic clarity, for the avoidance of 'duff terminology' — witness the language of Duff in *Landscape* — gives rise to a constant power struggle in Pinter's plays. In *The Dumb Waiter*, Gus and Ben, the two hired killers, actually fight over a terminological matter, arguing whether it is linguistically correct to say 'light the kettle' or 'light the gas' (I, 141–3), not unlike the linguistic purists who send letters to *The Times*. The battle is more restrained in *No Man's Land*, as Hirst and Spooner, two ostensible poets, pretend to believe that the 'salvation of the English language' lies with them (IV, 81). In *The Hothouse*, however, Roote makes it a deliberate point of contention that change is 'not *the* order of things, it's *in* the order of things' (p. 21), just as Edward and Flora tiff over whether bees 'bite' or 'sting' in the genteel world of *A Slight Ache* (I, 173); and A. and B. argue whether a sandwich man is likely to have 'headaches' or 'neckaches' in the revue sketch 'That's Your Trouble' (III,

227). In *Old Times* the futility of such word games seems even greater, for any failure to find *le mot juste* is quickly seized on as a sign of weakness. Deeley, irritated by Anna's continuing influence over his wife, quibbles famously with her somewhat archaic use of language, picking on words such as 'beguiling', 'lest' and 'gaze' as if their antiquatedness alone was sufficient proof of the antiquity of her involvement with his wife Kate (because Anna uses obsolete language, her affair with Kate must also be obsolete, or so Deeley's muddy logic seems to suggest).

*

In *The Caretaker* (1959), one of Pinter's most obscure plays and also one of his best, we are left in the dark from the outset. The opening scene has Mick silently looking around the pile of junk in his brother's room, and the initial question raised – and never fully resolved – is who is this man and what game is he playing? But it is not just Mick who plays games. It is Davies, after all, the nosy old man, who is asked 'What's the game?' as he is pinned to the floor by Mick in the brilliant *coup de théâtre* at the end of the first act (another astonishing 'curtain line', of which Pinter can be justifiably proud).

The Caretaker was Pinter's first great critical and commercial success on a London stage. Like many of the early plays, its subject is a room, and an outsider who threatens to disturb the peaceful sanctuary that this room represents. The room in this case is a humble bedsitter, part of a larger house which has other rooms 'out of commission' because they need 'a lot of doing to' (II, 21). The room is apparently owned by Mick, the breadwinner of the family, but it is currently lived in by his elder brother Aston who has been left mentally retarded, supposedly as a result of his experience in a psychiatric hospital. The outsider is Davies, a cantankerous old tramp who is invited to stay a while by Aston 'Till you . . . get yourself fixed up' (II, 25). Davies, however, abuses Aston's kindness and fails to ingratiate himself into the family; he even tries to play off first Aston, then Mick, against the other, but the fraternal bond

51

proves too strong and it is Davies who is eventually evicted at the end of the play.

One of the games that both Mick and Davies appear to be playing is a kind of hide-and-seek, a game that is actually very popular in this continually evasive world of Pinter's, where (ideally) all would rather hide than seek and be safe in the burrow of their own darkness, like an ostrich burying its head in the sand, or a child covering its eyes so as not to be seen. But there are seekers all around, and since there is always the chance of being found out it is often better to pretend to be the aggressor who seeks rather than the defendant who hides (attack being the best means of defence). In Pinter's plays, and in *The Caretaker* in particular, the rules of hide-and-seek allow each player a double role: each has to *hide* his sense of identity from the others, while *seeking* to find out more about these others in return. It is a particularly dangerous game, in Pinter's view, since it encompasses what they all try to keep away from – 'the danger of knowing, and of being known',[43] which is an 'alarming' prospect:

> I think that we communicate only too well, in our silence, in what is unsaid, and that what takes place is a continual evasion, desperate rearguard attempts to keep ourselves to ourselves. Communication is too alarming. To enter into someone else's life is too frightening. To disclose to others the poverty within us is too fearsome a possibility. (1, 15)

There are two *others* that have to be avoided: the *other* inside and the *other* outside. The former can be resisted by opting for cowardice and ignorance (of the self). Lies are necessary not only to misinform the *other* outside (survival being based on a policy of reciprocal misunderstanding) but also to misinform the *other* inside. To be honest means to be at the mercy of the world; or at the mercy of language (a frightening idea: to say 'I love you' and be forced to love!); or, even worse, at the mercy of ourselves – that part of ourselves we do everything to ignore. This drive towards self-ignorance is the one intellectual enterprise at which we excel. Fortunately we are helped by the fact that mirrors are 'deceptive' (as Bill says in *The Collection*; II, 146). In Pirandello's novel *One, No One and One Hundred Thousand*, Vitangelo Moscarda, shaving in the morning, realizes for the first time in his life that his nose is crooked. This just goes to show that mirrors have to be 'deceptive': they have either deceived him in the past, when he was thinking of himself as a straight-nosed individual; or they are deceiving him now, as he discovers the crooked nature of his nose. Vitangelo is thus faced with his *double*, like Golyadkin on the Fontanka Quay in Dostoevsky's great novel, but eventually he finds solace in the serene harbour of madness, where all opposites are reconciled. Rimbaud's frightening 'Je est un autre' ('I *is* another')[44] or Lacan's ironical 'The unconscious is the discourse of the Other'[45] require intellectual heroes who can think of these duplicities and face the consequences. Like us, Pinter's characters lack this boldness and continue to pretend to be themselves with thorough and impudent bad faith, because they know that their secrets are so well hidden that they themselves have forgotten what they are and where they are. And no one else is likely to dig them out.

The *other* outside has to be faced sooner or later, though, and this is why one plays hide-and-seek: the unknown entity represents (as in the blind Negro of *The Room* (to Rose) or the elusive Sally Gibbs in *Night School* (to Walter)) a direct threat to the stability of the individual. Whereas hiding comes naturally to Davies, seeking ('enter[ing] into someone else's life') is very much out of character. He does all he can to try to track Mick down in order to discover whether he poses him any threat, but Mick, a master of the will-o'-the-wisp technique, never lets himself be taken for granted in this way. He hides behind an array of different personae, defending the fortress of his identity with a display of masks that Davies finds puzzling. Is Mick, in due accordance with his name, being 'funny' or insincere ('taking the Mick')?[46] Davies can never tell, because Mick is a practised exponent of the tongue-in-cheek, and he also has an unsettling knack of shifting between different levels of phatic and rhetorical discourse. Davies's initial response to Mick is to admit 'I don't know you. I don't know who you are' (II, 39),

53

and, despite all his efforts to the contrary, he is none the wiser by the end of the play.

'Who are you?' is a question often asked, rarely answered, in the second definable phase of Pinter's writing (from around 1959 to 1961). It is the final whispered question asked by Edward in the mysterious presence of the matchseller in *A Slight Ache* (first performed in 1959). Harry likewise insists on asking 'Who is this?' when he receives an early morning call at the beginning of *The Collection* (1961). The most celebrated example, though – surprisingly explicit for Pinter – is the long speech delivered by Len in *The Dwarfs* (1960), of which perforce only an extract is given here:

> The point is, who are you? [. . .] What you are, or appear to be to me, or appear to be to you, changes so quickly, so horrifyingly, I certainly can't keep up with it and I'm damn sure you can't either. [. . .] You're the sum of so many reflections. How many reflections? Whose reflections? Is that what you consist of? (II, 111–12)

How can one justifiably accuse Pinter of 'deliberate mystification' when faced with a passage like this? This is even more embarrassingly honest than Aston's revelations to Davies about his experiences in the 'nuthouse' – as if all of a sudden the great poker player was beginning to show his hand. Many of the plays written by Pinter around this time are grinding meditations on the 'who you are' and 'what you are' questions. Len's speech summarizes Pinter's underlying belief in the difficulty, the impossibility even, of ever truly knowing anyone else. Though Mick remains obstinately in the shadows, he is not ill defined; he is well defined in his ill-definedness. His elusiveness is not a failure in Pinter's character portrayal, as some would have it, but a great theatrical invention. This is what Pinter has to say about ill-defined characters:

> A character on the stage who can present no convincing argument or information as to his past experience, his present behaviour or his aspirations, nor give a comprehensive analysis of his motives is as legitimate and as worthy of attention as one who, alarmingly, can do all these things. (I, 11)

To depict a shifty character, one can contrast him with a static, undeviating one. Mick and Aston, the two brothers, reinforce and complement each other's status in the play by being, on the surface, two opposite types: extrovert versus introvert, active versus passive, work-hungry versus work-shy, aggressive versus gentle, strong versus weak, and so on. In Pinterian terms, Aston is the sitting duck, because he leaves his defences open by talking revealingly about himself (unlike Mick, who talks only in order to confuse his opponent), first in the café where he 'talked too much' before being certified, and then with Davies in the long description of his ordeal in a psychiatric hospital, which allows the tramp to use this as evidence against him. (Although he admits to finding Aston a 'bit of a funny bloke' (II, 58), Davies seems on the verge of discovering that he is actually the most straightforward, the least cagey, of all of Pinter's characters.) Aston's insensitivity to the menace all around him is paradoxically symbolized in his statue of the Buddha (the Enlightened One), which, if forced to interpret, we would say becomes an emblem of his quiet charitableness and tolerance. By smashing the Buddha in the final act, Mick seems not only to want to make a dramatic impact on Davies (and the audience), but also to attempt to bring Aston out of his desensitized stupor. He has achieved his desired effect by the end of the play because, when Aston next appears, he 'sees the broken Buddha and looks at the pieces for a moment', then deliberately turns his back on Davies (which is a rejection of the old man by the young as final and tragic as King Hal's rejection of Falstaff at the end of *Henry IV, Part 2*).

Unlike Aston, Mick scents the danger represented by Davies's alien presence from the beginning, and moves to counteract it by immediately going on the offensive. The fact that Mick spends most of his time seeking (at one point, looking for the tramp in the dark with a buzzing electrolux; II, 54) and Davies hiding (even shying away beneath the bed-covers, by his own admission, pretending to be asleep but watching Aston with his 'eye on him all the time through the blanket'; II, 72) testifies to the superior skill and strength of the former, and the sheer cowardice of the latter. Whereas Mick is able to switch personae with consummate ease, Davies flounders under pressure when driven to the 'extreme edge of [his] living'[47] by Mick. He gives a series of unconvincing performances in his various identifying roles ('honourable tramp', 'honest friend', 'well-travelled man of experience', potential 'caretaker' and 'interior decorator'), and his unequal pairing with Mick often makes his efforts seem ridiculous. Yet, beneath the surface humour of his role, Davies is 'actually fighting a battle for his life', as the author himself points out.[48] He strives frantically to keep up a sense of appearances for fear of a kind of existentialist non-being (a fear reiterated by Lenny in *The Homecoming*, parodying his philosopher brother Teddy, as a concern for 'all this business of being and not-being'; III, 68).

Though his resources are somewhat limited, Davies still manages to find a few masquerading tricks up his sleeve. His main ploy is his use of stammer and equivocation, resorting to untrustworthiness whenever questioned. When he is asked if he is Welsh, for instance, he hedges round the issue by simply saying 'Well, I been around, you know . . .' (II, 34). He replies to each demand made of him in the same oblique manner, his resolution plainly being to be as unforthcoming as possible. He only once errs in giving particulars, when he specifies Sidcup as his proving-ground: 'If only I could get down to Sidcup! [. . .] I could prove everything' (II, 29). In the filmed version of the play (still to be generally released), this one slip almost proves fatal. Mick decides to call the old man's bluff by personally taking him down to Sidcup in his van – but, fortunately for Davies, they never actually get that far.[49]

By not giving anything away about himself – save for this one slip – one might think that Davies had successfully covered up his tracks (even to himself) and eluded Mick, the pursuing hunter. But, though Davies's ability to hide is masterly, Mick manages to seek him out by turning his very elusiveness against him. If Davies talks rubbish, even pretending not to remember the details of where he was born ('oh, it's a bit hard, like, to set your mind back . . . see what I mean . . . going back . . . a good way . . . lose a bit of track, like . . .'; II, 34), Mick is determined to outplay him at his own game. Thus we have the magnificent series of unrelated anecdotes, aimed at undermining Davies's already unstable existence, in which the colourless old man is likened to an impossibly colourful relation of Mick's, an 'uncle's brother' (a 'long-jump specialist' with a 'penchant for nuts'), as well as 'a bloke I once knew in Shoreditch' (who actually lived in Aldgate), whose life-history seems to consist of nothing but a topography of the drabbest London bus routes (II, 40–1).

Davies, hopelessly disorientated, has to resort to an alternative ploy in his battle for survival: he pretends to be someone else, disguising his 'true' identity under an assumed name (Bernard Jenkins). Mick, ever alert to chinks in another person's armour, plagues the tramp by repeatedly asking him 'What did you say your name was?', lingering on each syllable of each answer to make sure his suspicions are made perfectly clear ('Jen . . . kins'). He persists in his attack and eventually reduces the old man to the pitiful state of the *unnamable*, having ripped away all the masks that had only been assembled in haste. Davies's identity does not lie in Sidcup, as he so often claims, but in his collection of evasive *fronts* (as Erving Goffman would put it). Once these are broken through, the 'poverty within us', mentioned by Pinter, becomes nakedly manifest in Davies's case. The shattering of his *fronts* is tantamount to an existential annihilation, which is even more dramatic than the violent death of the tramp (Pinter claims that this was his original idea in writing the play).[50] The brothers unite with a smile in denying him any right to exist, and Aston's deliberate ignoring of the old man signifies that Mick has at last reclaimed him to his protective fold.

Despite the viciousness of Davies, the dullness of Aston and certain traits of motiveless malignity in Mick, *The Caretaker* is finally a play about love: brotherly love. When Pinter was recently asked about the meaning of the faint smiling between the two brothers in the final scene, he surprised everybody present, first of all by answering such an 'impertinent' question and then by the outrageousness of his answer: 'I think it's a smile that they love each other.'[51] If one considers that Pinter

57

has also said, in another lapse of avowed critical introspection, that *The Homecoming* too is a play 'about love and lack of love',[52] then one might be tempted to make a thorough revaluation of these plays – not in terms of 'menace' or the absurd, but in terms of frustration of emotion and deprivation of love.

5

CRITICAL GAMES:
'THE HOMECOMING'

To reinterpret *The Homecoming* solely in terms of 'love' and 'frustrated emotion' would, however, be a wasted exercise. The play is too rich a brew to be reduced to a single flavour. Like many mysterious plays in our theatrical canon (notably, *Hamlet*), *The Homecoming* is a magnet that attracts new interpretations which serve to dismember the text. The original text does not exist any longer, buried as it is under the multiple readings that have submerged it. In the same way that *Hamlet* can never free itself from the Oedipal transcriptions that Sigmund Freud and Ernst Jones have written upon the Shakespearian palimpsest, *The Homecoming* is forced to drag behind it the 'soap opera' interpretations that Martin Esslin has elicited from the Pinterian script (about which, more anon). The text's dismemberment – which is also the text's enrichment – is the price that Pinter has had to pay for the overwhelming success of *The Homecoming* both at home and abroad.

The Caretaker ran for a year in the West End of London, but it received a cool audience reception in New York when it was transferred to Broadway in 1961. *The Homecoming* (first performed in 1965) was Pinter's next major stage play – following on from some experimental and highly successful work in both television (*Night School*, *The Collection*, *The Lover*, *Tea Party*) and the cinema (*The Servant*, a filmed version of *The Caretaker* known as *The Guest* in the USA, and *The Pumpkin Eater*). Though it was a long time in coming, it proved to be the great breakthrough in America, winning the Tony Award for the best play on Broadway in 1967 with virtually the same members of the Royal Shakespeare Company who had earlier monopolized the Aldwych Theatre in the West End for over a year and a half.

In spite of Pinter's legendary spare style, economical dialogue and bare plot, the early plays had been too rich, the playwright being unable to deny himself the joys of superfluity. He later admitted that both 'The Birthday Party and The Caretaker have too much writing. . . . I want to iron it down, eliminate things.'[53] The Lulu episode is presumably the dispensable section in The Birthday Party, since it seems to belong to a different – and earlier – kind of play, and does not contribute to the main plot. It is more difficult to locate what could be eliminated in The Caretaker, unless Pinter was thinking of Aston's confessional monologue which, though amply successful, has a somewhat odd position in the play, forcing the audience into an excessive sympathy for the character. In The Homecoming all the frivolities of the plot are eliminated. No longer 'two people in a room', as in the earlier theatrical experiments, the play features four male people in a house who have to withstand the homecoming of the couple returning from America. Two older brothers, Max the butcher and Sam the chauffeur, and the younger fraternity, Lenny the pimp and Joey the boxer, attend the unexpected return of Teddy, their prodigal son/nephew/brother, who has become a successful academic at an American university in his six years' absence from the house. In the meantime Teddy has married Ruth, his London-born wife, who has fathered him three sons (like Jessie, Max's late wife), and this completes the symmetrical patterning of the play's two familial groupings. Pinter has indeed remarked that the 'only play which gets remotely near to a structural entity which satisfies me is The Homecoming', and 'to get the structure right', as he puts it, has always been his major dramatic concern.[54]

The four main protagonists (the father and son, Max and Lenny; the husband and wife, Teddy and Ruth) engage in the course of the play in a series of pitched verbal battles, leading towards the family's absorption of the alien body, Ruth, who finally agrees to desert her own American family and become a prostitute. The battles remain constrained at a purely verbal level, actual violence being only hinted at in Lenny's threatening speeches and resorted to in moments of sheer desperation by the weakest of the foursome, Max. To resort to violence is to acknowledge defeat, for *The Homecoming* is essentially a play about language – about articulating a language and being articulated by a language. In Pinter's world, social control lies ultimately in the power to impose one's language on another. Hitler knew this well: if you succeed in putting the words *Übermensch* and *Herrenvolk* into other people's mouths, then your battle is already won. Mick in *The Caretaker* imposes his language on Davies and thus defeats him (insisting at one point 'I don't call it funny', to which Davies cravenly agrees 'Nor me'; II, 59). In *A Slight Ache*, on the other hand, Edward attempts to impose his sophisticated language on the match-seller but fails, exasperated by the unbreachable barrier of silence ('Did you say something? (*Pause.*) Anything?'; I, 194).

In *The Homecoming*, where linguistic control is even more clearly the name of the game, Max and Teddy fail where Lenny and Ruth so obviously succeed (though at the end Ruth seems the eventual overall winner). Teddy cannot impose his utopian vision of America on Ruth because what is for him an ivory tower, a shrine of sanitation ('It's so clean there'), is for her a place of sterility, a barren wasteland ('It's all rock. And sand'; III, 69–70). Max, for his part, tries to impose himself upon his household by adopting a hybrid language of physical vitalism (denied by his physical decadence), carnal brutality (undermined by his querulous complaints) and aggressive sentimentality. 'I always had the smell of a good horse. I could smell him' (III, 26), he boasts, while showing clear signs of his ignorance of the turf. 'I worked as a butcher all my life, using the chopper and the slab, the slab, you know what I mean, the chopper and the slab!' (III, 63), he blurts out, while attempting to present himself as a mild and considerate family man. 'Every single bit of the moral code they live by – was taught to them by their mother. And she had a heart to go with it. What a heart.

[. . .] That woman was the backbone to this family' (III, 62), he gushes, while at the same time pouring abuse over his unfortunate spouse. Unlike Goldberg in *The Birthday Party*, whose speech mannerisms he sometimes echoes, Max fails to convince others of the gift of his gab and, like Teddy, is finally defeated by his linguistic incompetence. Prone to make connective slips, he often says quite another thing from what he means, the most unfortunate example being the celebrated 'I've never had a whore under this roof before. Ever since your mother died' (III, 58). Teddy also displays this trait, welcoming Ruth to the silent house by claiming ominously that his family are 'not ogres' (III, 39).

All this points to the wide discrepancy between their linguistic competence and performance, between their intention and the results. Unlike their counterparts, Ruth and Lenny, neither Max nor Teddy knows how to tell a story. When Teddy is invited to comment on 'a certain logical incoherence in the central affirmations of Christian theism' (Lenny's bold inroad into his brother's territory), he declines to take up the bait and replies laconically and cowardly: 'That question doesn't fall within my province' (III, 67). Similarly, when Max tries to relate a racing anecdote to Lenny, he predictably fails to maintain any kind of narrative flow: 'Many times I was offered the job – you know, a proper post, by the Duke of . . . I forget his name . . . one of the Dukes' (III, 26). Max is so used to linguistic defeats that, by the final scene of the play, he cannot believe that his earlier suggestion, 'Maybe we should keep her' (III, 85), has turned true – that Ruth is staying for real:

Lenny, do you think she understands . . . [. . .] What . . . what . . . what . . . we're getting at? What . . . we've got in mind? Do you think she's got it clear? (*Pause.*) I don't think she's got it clear. (*Pause.*) You understand what I mean? Listen, I've got a funny idea she'll do the dirty on us, you want to bet? She'll use us, she'll make use of us, I can tell you! I can smell it! You want to bet? (III, 97)

Within the context of the play, he may be quite right (Ruth might very well make use of them), but his stammering indicates insecurity. His request for a kiss is a defiance of his senile impotence, but also a request for factual confirmation of his linguistic triumph (if she kisses him, then his earlier words will have come true: his language will have for once controlled reality).

Unlike Max and Teddy, Lenny remains in full control of the language until he finds an even better player than himself. Perverse as it may seem, Lenny is a supreme conversationalist, a great teller of (tall) stories. His generous bestowing of trivial information about the clock, or his threatening warning about his beating up of both young and old women, is above all an attempt to impose upon Ruth his own linguistic dominance. It is the opposite of plagiarism. The plagiarist takes and uses another person's language as his own; the anti-plagiarist, or plagiarist in reverse, forces his own language upon other people. Lenny, like Mick in *The Caretaker*, aspires to be an anti-plagiarist by setting the tone, style and subject-matter of the conversation. He wants to be able to select the entire grammar and vocabulary of every verbal exchange. For him – as for all manipulating characters in Pinter – language reigns supreme. When Ruth asks him 'How did you know she [i.e. the prostitute] was diseased?', he replies 'How did I know? (*Pause.*) I decided she was' (III, 47): in the context this becomes the equivalent of 'I *said* she was'. The real threat is not physical but linguistic. Instead of gagging people, you un-gag them, trying to insinuate a way into the private stronghold of their language (as Iago does so magnificently in *Othello*); it is not so much a case of taking the words out of people's mouths as putting words *into* their mouths: a sort of ventriloquist's trick.

The fight for possession of the tongue is in opposition to the fight for possession of the soul. In fact, the playwright seems determined to stamp out the inner world of the soul, of intimate thoughts, of memories and desires. Yet no matter how hard he fights against this private realm (the realm of private language which Wittgenstein repudiates in the *Investigations*) it always perversely re-emerges. Everything happens on the surface, at skin level; but behind the skin there is the skull, and inside the skull there are ideas, emotions, feelings, amorous longings. In other words, people continue against all odds to be 'a bit inner'. Pinter is the only writer who has transformed psychological depth and inwardness into an insult. Here are Albert's friends, in *A Night Out*, talking about his 'inner life':

KEDGE. He's a bit deep really, isn't he?
SEELEY. Yes, he's a bit deep.

> *Pause.*

KEDGE. Secretive.
SEELEY (*irritably*). What do you mean, secretive? What are you talking about?
KEDGE. I was just saying he was secretive.
SEELEY. What are you talking about? What do you mean, he's secretive?
KEDGE. You said yourself he was deep.
SEELEY. I said he was deep. I didn't say he was secretive! (I, 214)

Davies in *The Caretaker* is horrified at the idea of dreams ('Dreaming? [. . .] I don't dream. I've never dreamed'; II, 31), because dreams would emerge from an inner world, outside the safe control of the tactical language of evasion, which is his only means of defence. But the sworn enemy of any form of *internal* life is Lenny, who wants to know whether Ruth's *proposal* is a *proposal*, leaving no margin for unexpressed desires or intentions. In the tense exchange with Teddy ('taking the piss' out of him, in Peter Hall's apt definition of the mood of the play[55]) Lenny accuses his brother of the ultimate sin: having a life inside. 'Mind you, I will say you do seem to have grown a bit sulky [. . .]. *A bit inner*. A bit less forthcoming' (III, 80; our italics). The adjective *inner* becomes truly offensive, since *innerness* is a defiance of the unwritten laws of common behaviour which require that one should never say or think anything related to *inner* life. Teddy dares to challenge the conventions of dishonest decency, the superficial reality of any relationship in the play, by having an *inner* life which is inaccessible to the others. And in his cruel exchange with Max about his own conception Lenny mocks the fact that there could be an emotional or sentimental background – an *inner* motion – behind the copulative act that generated him. The target is always the *inner* life.

Lenny finds his match when faced with Ruth. The two have a lot in common, even sharing the same world of make-believe, as witness their joint fantasizing about the Italian campaign. Lenny: 'if I'd been a soldier in the last war [. . .] I'd probably have found myself in Venice' (III, 46). Ruth, in a different scene: 'But if I'd been a nurse in the Italian campaign I would have been there before' (III, 71). In their world, language controls reality and not vice versa. But Ruth has the advantage over Lenny in having sex at her disposal – a much-demanded commodity in the household of *The Homecoming*. Sex is for her an aggressive weapon of seduction which she uses, in conjunction with her linguistic skill, to tantalize her opponent: 'Have a sip from my glass. [. . .] Lie on the floor. Go on. I'll pour it down your throat' (III, 50; the latter remark being a threat as well as a lure). By saying 'I'll take you', she is not 'making . . . some kind of proposal' but putting herself in the dominant position of the taker, not the taken one. She thus reduces Lenny to sheepish confusion: 'What was that supposed to be?' he begs (III, 51). She continues the same combined assault of linguistic and sexual power into the second act when she shatters the metaphysical discussion about the meaning of the word 'table' ('philosophically speaking'; III, 68) with a pincer attack – playing on the word *leg* and the thing *leg*, on the word *lips* and the thing *lips*, through which the words come to life; forcing *signifier* and *signified* to collaborate in order to ensure her total victory over her male onlookers:

> Don't be too sure though. You've forgotten something. Look at me. I . . . move my leg. That's all it is. But I wear . . . underwear . . . which moves with me . . . it . . . captures your attention. Perhaps you misinterpret. The action is simple. It's a leg . . . moving. My lips move. Why don't you restrict . . . your observations to that? Perhaps the fact that they move is more significant . . . than the words which come through them. (III, 68–9)

*

This is just one way of looking at the text. There have been many others, and doubtless there will continue to be many more. As Peter Hall has pointed out, *The Homecoming* is a play that does not display seven but an infinite number of types of ambiguity.[56] Some of the readings that have been offered we feel broadly in sympathy with (Max as a modern King Lear suffering from a lifetime deprivation of love, Lenny and Ruth as a downgraded gay couple from a Restoration comedy of manners, etc.).[57] Others we feel out of sympathy with, at times wildly so (orthodox Freudian interpretations via the dream work, ritualistic and ceremonial readings via *The Golden Bough*, moralistic readings, etc.).[58] Of all the many interpretations, the most convincing for us is the one given by Irving Wardle (the drama critic of *The Times*), whose anthropological reading has been much echoed by younger critics. For Wardle, *The Homecoming* articulates a bestial fight for territory and supremacy with the characters resorting to basic animalistic defences such as fight, flight and mimetism in order to survive.[59] The bestial metaphor, it is believed, was discreetly present ever since Pinter's earliest works, but it became explicit in *The Homecoming*, where even timid creatures such as Sam behave like animals (Sam is the supposed 'weakling of the pack', and as such is mercilessly eliminated). It is consequently a play to be understood, if at all, in terms of what Wardle calls its 'territorial struggle'. Max is not the paterfamilias but the male hunter 'going all over the country to find meat' (III, 62), the leader of the herd which is going to be ousted by the young males. It is not a play that celebrates or ridicules the homecoming of Teddy, who becomes a marginal figure, but of Ruth who gives her love (i.e. her body) to the male with the 'best piece of property'. She has sex to offer, they have territory – and by the laws of the jungle it seems a perfectly equitable exchange (as suggested in Chapter 2, a similar exchange takes place in *The Basement*, Pinter's television play of 1966, in the course of which Law loses his territory but gets the girl). America, a desert populated by insects, was not suited to Ruth's animal instincts. She needs the comparative filth of London's mean streets, the brawls of uncivilized dwellings, the stench of low life, in order to prosper. To conquer her natural habitat she has to abandon Teddy, who goes 'limp' like Desmond Morris's naked ape, and choose the male who has most to offer in return for her sexual wares. Her husband only needs her for her mind (to help him with his lectures), but the others' needs are far greater, for it is her body they want. Agreeing to offer her sex to household and stranger alike, Ruth is not captive but queen bee, the triumphant conqueror of swarm and hive.[60]

By presenting our own 'linguistic' interpretation side by side with Wardle's 'anthropological' one, we are not claiming any special privileged position for either. Neither seems to us excessively harmful to the text; and in any case it is our belief that any hierarchical arrangement ought not to be geared towards a process of elimination. A great play, such as *The Homecoming*, is strong enough to take upon itself all sorts of interpretations, even the most ludicrous. A plurality of readings has to be encouraged, so as to test the play's resistance. Not all interpretations have the same credibility, but, theoretically, they all have the same epistemological standing (save for those which have no evidential grounding in the text). Two readings can even be quite contradictory and still have equal merit. Depending on how you look at it, *The Homecoming* can, for instance, be seen as both a play tainted by misogynism, and one imbued with feminist values.

From one perspective, it can be seen as a meditation on the horrors of femalehood, taking its inspiration from Strindberg (a playwright who seems to have influenced Pinter). Everyone can be seen to hate women in this play, though the author himself appears neutral with respect to the characters' rampant misogyny. Max is haunted by the memory of his 'slutbitch' wife, and immediately qualifies the new female visitor as a 'dirty tart' and 'smelly scrubber' (III, 57). Lenny's living seems to depend on psychological exploitation of, and physical threat against, women. The moronic Joey screws mechanically, as if making love were just another 'demolition job', and is incapable of understanding the need for (contraceptive) protection of the girls he rapes. Teddy treats his wife as a less than precious commodity, appreciating neither her needs nor her point of view ('The last thing I want is a breath of air. Why do you want a breath of air?'; III, 40). The only person not openly hostile to women, if not particularly sympathetic, is Sam, and he is protected from the endemic disease of women-hating by his homosexuality ('You'd bend over for half a dollar on Black-friars Bridge.[. . .] For two bob and a toffee apple'; III, 64). Having these inclinations, he is saved the unnecessary bother of hating women, who prove no threat to him. The other men of the family do not need a woman in the house but a 'nice feminine girl' (III, 65) – that is, a girl prepared to fulfil her supposed feminine duties: to kiss, to be screwed, to be 'wide open', not to be a 'tease', to 'go the whole hog', to deliver the 'gravy' (and, in the process, to be 'clumped', to be taken 'over the rubble', to be given a 'short-arm jab to the belly').

Going 'the whole hog' (as Lenny and Joey so delightfully put it; III, 82 and *passim*) raises the problem of pregnancy, hence of fatherhood. Who is the father of whom? Sam suggests that Max's closest friend, the legendary McGregor, terror of the West End, 'had Jessie in the back of [his] cab' (III, 94), casting doubt on the legitimacy of one, or perhaps all, of the 'three fine grown-up lads' (III, 61). But who is the bastard? Lenny pursues the same line of inquiry in his cruel teasing of his father:

> That night . . . you know . . . the night you got me . . . [. . .] what was it like? Eh? [. . .] What was the background to it? I mean, I want to know the real facts about my back-ground.[. . .] It's a question long overdue, from my point of view, but as we happen to be passing the time of day here tonight I thought I'd pop it to you. (III, 52)

Max's savage reply, 'You'll drown in your own blood' (III, 52), may be an indication of his present anger and past jealousy. Or, playing the amateur psychoanalysts for a moment, we could interpret this 'drowning in blood' as wishful thinking: the bastard son deserves to be an aborted foetus which drowns in the mother's menstrual blood. Lenny, seemingly imperturb-able as ever, insists: 'I should have asked my dear mother. Why didn't I ask my dear mother?' (III, 53). By daring to hint at the unaskable question, *The Homecoming* resembles Strindberg's

Storm Weather (*Oväder*), a play that for three long scenes hints at but never faces the crucial problem of whether the prematurely senile protagonist is the legitimate father of the child.

Considered from another angle, *The Homecoming* can be seen to pursue, contradictorily, a feminist line, and the clue here is John Fowles's novel *The French Lieutenant's Woman*, an ardently pro-feminist text for which Pinter has written a screenplay (see Chapter 8). Viewed in this light, the plot of *The Homecoming* could be retold along the following lines. Ruth and her husband return to London, where Teddy's father and brothers live. She abandons her husband so as to gain her freedom, for which she barters with the hard weaponry of her sex. Sex has no hold on her philosophical spouse, whose post-doctoral demands require only a bourgeois wife or Ibsenesque 'doll'. But it gives her real control over the rest of the household (again, Sam apart), when it is used ruthlessly, as it is with Lenny: 'If you take the glass . . . I'll take you' (III, 50). She gains her freedom just as Sarah Woodruff achieves her heroical independence in *The French Lieutenant's Woman* – by 'marrying shame' (a key phrase in Fowles's novel). By accepting to be in popular imagination the French Lieutenant's whore, and in real life Charles's mistress (even for a single night), Sarah becomes liberated as a woman, freed from the shackles of her institutionalized role as governess. By agreeing to satisfy the household's sexual needs (while driving a hard bargain and remaining a 'tease'), Ruth also gains a paradoxical independence, since by becoming a whore she is able to break free from the academic straitjacket of the philosopher's lowly wife. With opposite voices and diverging means, Sarah and Ruth affirm their joint intention not to keep to the rules of a game that have been set by males. (For a similar view on a broad historical canvas, see Angela Carter's *The Sadeian Woman*, where the Sadeian predestined victim, the woman, becomes liberated through the breaking of stereotypes.) Far from being a misogynist play, *The Homecoming* can be seen as a powerful plea for feminine and feminist independence.

All this goes to prove Hall's point that *The Homecoming* is as multifaceted as a diamond, and that 'any proposition we draw from one side of the play we can contradict or modify by a proposition from some other side'.[61] Or, as Mick remarks of Davies in *The Caretaker*, in an uncharacteristically astute comment that could apply equally well to any of Pinter's own plays: 'Honest. I can take nothing you say at face value. *Every word you speak is open to any number of different interpretations*. Most of what you say is lies' (II, 82; our italics).

Yet critics have moodily echoed Mick's sentiments and attempted to close Pinter down by providing crude *explications* of his texts, aiming towards the hermeneutical paradise, where one is free to say: 'What the play really means is . . .' The author himself has retorted sharply to this reductionist approach by suggesting that the singleminded search for clear-cut meanings is hopeless:

> meaning begins in the words, in the action, continues in your head, and ends nowhere. There is no end to meaning. Meaning which is resolved, parcelled, labelled and ready for export is dead, impertinent and meaningless.[62]

The adjective 'impertinent'[63] seems to us particularly important here, because, if meaning is an impertinence, pertinence must lie somewhere else – perhaps in formal values and dramatic strategies.

Critics have, however, persisted in their impertinence, searching for the terminal point where meaning stops and tarries, parcelling the plays up in any number of different guises. Indeed, the temptation to nail Pinter down is so great that we have not only bordered on doing so but have ourselves entered this forbidden zone (of interpretation) on a number of errant occasions. The tendency is to treat Pinter's characters – compulsive, conniving liars every one of them – as if they were as trustworthy as the Houyhnhnms in *Gulliver's Travels*, those saintly equine creatures incapable of lying. Critics seem to deny their role as unbelievers. No matter how improbable the statement in the play, how implausible the situation, how extravagant the motivation, how tall the story, honourable critics ponderously assess and discuss the declarations of the Pinterian character as if they were reliable. Spooner (in *No*

70

Man's Land) 'is acquainted with the impeccably aristocratic Lord Lancer. He is able to organize a poetry reading for Hirst that will include . . . a dinner party at a fine Indian restaurant' (Lucina Paquet Gabbard). 'It is made quite clear by Ruth [in *The Homecoming*] that when Teddy met her and married her she was a nude photographic model – and this is widely known as a euphemism for a prostitute' (Martin Esslin). Mick (in *The Caretaker*) 'had believed Davies to be an interior decorator' (Nigel Alexander).[64] In all these instances, critics give the Pinterian hero a credit that he does not deserve and does not require. We are not necessarily supposed to believe that Spooner is acquainted with Lord Lancer, or that Ruth was a prostitute; least of all are we expected to believe that Mick believed that Davies was an interior decorator (!). All we know is that there are characters who are making these statements: not that these statements are valid.

Of all the critics, Martin Esslin is perhaps the most consistently guilty of 'pigeonholing Pinter'[65] and taking his heroes at their word. His attempt to collate Pinter with Beckett, Ionesco *et al.* under the immensely successful banner of 'The Theatre of the Absurd' is an impressive example of literary categorization, monumentally ill directed, in our view. He is, we believe, at once the most perceptive of Pinter's critics and the playwright's worst enemy. On the one hand, he recognizes the need to maintain the proper sense of pluralistic ambiguity in his readings, and avoids the common mistake of demanding an either/ or simplification from his plays when the author himself has always insisted on the necessity of an optional and/or (Pinter has said: 'A thing is not necessarily either true or false; it can be both true and false'; i, 11). At the same time, however, he appears to want to seal what he calls the 'open wound' in Pinter's plays – that which Pinter leaves deliberately unexplained. *The Homecoming* has particularly suffered from his 'realistic' interpretations in which the text is made to seem 'credible' (Ruth as a nymphomaniac; Jessie as an immoral woman; Teddy worried about the 'gossip-ridden campus'; Ruth unwilling to go the whole way with Joey because she wants to avoid a 'tedious or unsatisfactory sexual rela-

71

tionship', etc.).[66] This is just one step away from some of the most ludicrous positivist approaches. 'Why does she do it?' muses one critic who wouldn't bat an eyelid if faced with Clytemnestra's behaviour, Medea's naughtiness or Lady Macbeth's impropriety. Why does she 'choose to surrender her most respectable, comfortable, secure and altogether enviable life?' (the plaintiff, we can assure our readers, is not one of the Stepford wives).[67] Or consider the final scene when Ruth stops to bid Teddy a not so fond farewell with the words 'Eddie . . . Don't become a stranger.' In the context that Esslin put this in, the evident cliché is to be construed literally as some kind of desperate lament on Ruth's part (for her lost innocence; for the hard 9 p.m. to 5 a.m. life she has in front of her; for the innocent lambs left to the care of a forgetful father who won't teach them proper dental care and prayers before beddy-byes). In Esslin's interpretations, the play, as we have already suggested, becomes little more than soap opera. He tries to satisfy a craving for comprehension (whatever that word might mean) to meet a critical requirement that was once vociferously demanded by the audiences (though not any longer, we believe; like Picasso's, or Stravinsky's, or Joyce's, Pinter's outrage has become the norm of respectability). Worthy though this aim might seem, he does this in spite of the fact that easy access to the text is explicitly denied us by the author: 'The desire for verification is . . . understandable but cannot always be satisfied' (I, 11).

As implied by this last quotation, the philosophical core at the heart of interpretative criticism is connected with verificationism and the so-called Vienna School of logical positivism (the school that Stoppard exposes to ridicule in *Jumpers*). Positivism aims to compress, to clarify all areas of discourse. A statement, according to this view, has to be analytically true or empirically verifiable. If it is neither of these, it is considered not to concord with the 'verificationist principle' and is deemed 'factually insignificant' (in the words of A. J. Ayer:[68] we are, of course, generalizing greatly). With Ogden and Richards's *The Meaning of Meaning* and the anti-intentionalist school of New Criticism, the verificationist ethos invaded the literary field

72

with the imperious demands of a new creed. But these demands, though 'understandable' and well intentioned, 'cannot
always be satisfied' by the dramatist. In one of his most playful
moments, Pinter even allowed himself an oblique jibe at the
impossibility of their aim:

> JOHN. Children seem to mean a great deal to their parents,
> I've noticed. Though I've often wondered what 'a great
> deal' means.
>
> TOM. I've often wondered what 'mean' means. (*Tea Party*;
> III, 115)

6

ENDGAMES:
A PERIOD OF TRANSITION

The Homecoming brought in its wake a flood of critical outpourings. Comparatively little had been written on Pinter before, and there has been comparatively little written since. Critics had seemed wholly bemused, before 1965, by the daunting task of trying to come to terms with the absurd phenomenon of 'Puzzling Pinter'.[69] When *The Birthday Party* opened in England just seven years earlier, it had met with almost total confusion, the reviewer of the *Manchester Guardian* typifying the general complaint with his defiant comment: 'What all this means, only Mr Pinter knows.'[70] Nor did the passing of time necessarily bring any greater understanding, and it took the advent of such a richly complex play as *The Homecoming* to inaugurate feverish attempts to tie Pinter down to precise 'solutions' – attempts at interpretation, some of which, as we have suggested, were perhaps misguided.

As if in reaction to this sudden burst of critical energy expended on *The Homecoming*, there was subsequently a period of sustained silence from both Pinter and his critics alike. Normally a prolific writer, Pinter did not write another full-length play for six years. He himself attributed this time of creative stagnation to the fact that 'When I was younger, my writing was free – words poured out of me onto the paper. Now [in 1968] my writing tends to be careful – constipated.'[71] This is not to say that he remained idle. He wrote two television plays for the BBC, *Tea Party* and *The Basement* – which renewed the critics' demands for 'explanation', the (London) *Evening News* reporter dismissing them both with the frank confession 'Mr Pinter's Puzzles Leave Me Guessing'[72] – and he also produced some further work in the cinema, including the scripts for *The Quiller Memorandum*, *Accident* and *The Go-Between*. But, when he at last got down to what he evidently believes to be the 'serious' business of writing for the theatre, the results were as surprising as they were long awaited. After a brief struggle with the Lord Chamberlain's Office over an alleged obscenity, *Landscape* appeared in 1969 as part of a one-act double bill with *Silence* at the Aldwych Theatre in London. Immediately it became clear that new ground was being broken. Indeed, one reason for the surprising lull in critical response to Pinter's most recent work may have been the abrupt change of direction and intent that these later plays represent, which has puzzled many an unsuspecting critic grown used to the 'Pinteresque' from Pinter.

Landscape and *Silence* accentuate Pinter's great indebtedness to his acknowledged mentor, Samuel Beckett, whom Pinter has described very simply as 'the greatest writer of our time'.[73] The sets in these plays are noticeably barer than anything seen in Pinter previously. Though his characters are comfortably installed in chairs and not ensconced, as in much of Beckett, in urns or dustbins, or buried in mounds of earth, a sense of stillness yet prevails. Movement on the stage is kept to a minimum. Characters are reduced to talking heads with wagging tongues, their ears receptive only to the sound of their own voices. In place of the typical mumblings of inarticulates like Davies in *The Caretaker*, we now have moments of intense lyricism, made pathetic by the isolation of the speakers. Audiences were struck by the austerity of the two new plays which gives them their distinctive Beckettian feel. Whereas *The Caretaker*'s cluttered bedsitter recalls the fetishism of commodities in Ionesco's *The New Tenant*, *Landscape* and *Silence* are more reminiscent of the bleakness of *Waiting for Godot* with its stark setting: 'A country road. A tree.'

Pinter declared his determination, following *The Homecoming*, to get away from his constantly pressing image of two

75

people in a room – 'this bunch of people who opened doors and came in and went out'. *Landscape* and *Silence*, he felt, were 'in a very different form. There isn't any menace at all.'[74] The basic device of the early 'comedies of menace' was the opening of a door and the entrance into a room. People from the outside world were threatening the temporary sanctuary of Rose in *The Room*, the safe digs where Stanley had taken refuge in *The Birthday Party*, the privacy of the English home-as-castle in *A Slight Ache*. But the external 'menace' seems to have largely disappeared in many of the later plays – or perhaps it has been deliberately subdued. In some respects it is interiorized, the characters being threatened by their ability to think, to remember, to fantasize, to hope – akin to the convoluted series of interior monologues that comprise Beckett's famous trilogy of novels. It seems that Pinter has grown tired of playing the bridging games that had characterized his earlier attempts in the theatre. In this he mirrors Beckett's own dramatic evolution, from the active game-playing of Estragon and Vladimir in *Godot* to the bored stalemating of Hamm and Clov in *Endgame*. In Pinter's early plays, up to and including *The Homecoming*, though there is no lasting communication between characters, they manage stumblingly to interact (like Estragon and Vladimir) through the evasive medium of playing games. With the onset of plays like *Landscape* and *Silence*, however, even this slender means of interaction breaks down, and the gap between one character and another grows into a chasm that no game can properly bridge.

In the Royal Shakespeare Company's production of *Landscape* in 1969, this chasm was actually illustrated by a split in John Bury's set which physically divided the two characters. This had seemed appropriate in the light of Pinter's uncharacteristically specific stage-directions, which ask Duff to refer normally to Beth though he does not hear her; while Beth, for her part, 'never looks at Duff, and does not appear to hear his voice' (III, 175). One has only to compare the absolute gulf between these two, presumably husband and wife, with the final tableau in *The Homecoming* – which has the three male predators, Lenny, Joey and Max, crowding around Ruth as she 'sits relaxed on her chair' – to see how even more desperate the situation has become in *Landscape*. This feeling of immense isolation is recaptured in *Silence*, where the characters occupy another divided stage, the set consisting of just three chairs: 'A chair in each area' (III, 200). The respective ages of the three characters – Rumsey is forty, Bates 'in his middle thirties', and Ellen 'in her twenties' – suggests that there is even a temporal void between them, a generation gap writ large with decades of indifference to separate them.

The logical development of this move towards seclusion and segregation is *Monologue*, another one-act play (produced by Pinter in 1973), which dramatizes a form of solitaire (after the fashion, perhaps, of Beckett's *Krapp's Last Tape* and his recent novella, *Company*). The Man who recites the monologue appears at first to be merrily chatting away to friends, but in the BBC television production we soon see that he is in fact 'alone in a chair' and 'refers to another chair, which is empty'. As has been pointed out,[75] a possible dramatic source for this frightening effect is Ionesco's *The Chairs*, where the old couple and the orator address a stage audience of empty chairs. This in turn looks back to Pirandello's short story *Professor Lamis's Vengeance*, in which the short-sighted university professor gives his lecture in a hall where each chair is occupied by a mackintosh.

Pinter appears to have come latterly to the logical impasse of *Endgame*, the *ultima Thule* of man's alienation in modern drama, where everyone lives 'pretty much alone'.[76] The particular endgame that Pinter seems to have alighted on is a sort of round game known popularly as 'consequences', a parlour game which in Pinter's plays actually promotes isolation rather than conviviality (as it does in Evelyn Waugh's *Black Mischief*, where the game is played). The *Collins English Dictionary* describes 'consequences' as 'British, a game in which each player writes down a part of the story, hands over the paper, and passes it on to another player who continues the story. After several stages, the resulting (nonsensical) stories are read out.' The surrealists played a similar game known as *cadavres exquis*, a mischievous jumbling up of words to form arbitrary poetry, but they were aiming to reach that deep level of a collective unconscious where the 'spirit' of the group could claim control over the aspirations of the individual. Pinter shares no such illusions of any mental or spiritual cognateness. His later plays follow instead the fractured pattern of 'consequences' by having each of the characters recall his or her memory, tell his or her side of the story, which is then followed, in sporadic turn, by each of the versions of all the others. The plays are then assembled out of a mismatch of all these various parts – a sequentially nonsensical jumble which can still be pieced together, if only in part, by the most observant of spectators or the most assiduous of readers.

It is this desolate game that provides the basic metaphor for the stories in much of Pinter's latest work. Its roots can be traced back to the conflicting 'truths' of a comparatively early play, *The Collection* (1961). Bill and Stella, the two hypothetical philanderers, give differing accounts of what happened or did not happen one night in Leeds, leaving their respective partners and the audience to decide which, if any, of their versions is correct. 'Consequences' is also the basis for the conflicting reminiscences in plays like *Old Times* (1970) and *No Man's Land* (1974), where no one's memory of an incident ever seems to tally with anyone else's. It is particularly noticeable in the revue sketch 'Night' (1969), where a middle-aged couple try to recall their first sexual encounter only to find their memories playing peculiar tricks on them. Comparing their two accounts, which combined seem 'nonsensical', it becomes clear that each remembers a very different encounter (just as in the popular song 'Ah yes, I remember it well!', from the film *Gigi*, Maurice Chevalier nostalgically remembers his wedding day only to have his recollections flatly contradicted by his screen wife, Hermione Gingold[77]).

Like many sceptical thinkers of the twentieth century, Pinter has begun to explore the suggestion that there is no such thing as a fixed, objective reality. He has long bordered on this area of relativism – witness Max's insistence on knowing 'From what point of view?' in *The Homecoming* (III, 29) – and he anticipated the later change of direction in his theatrical practice in an early comment in 1962, claiming that what we *think* of as reality is actually no more than a series of subjective views which very rarely coincide:

> We will all interpret a common experience quite differently, though we prefer to subscribe to the view that there's a shared common ground, a known ground. I think there's a shared common ground all right, but that it's more like a quicksand. Because 'reality' is quite a strong firm word we tend to think, or to hope, that the state to which it refers is equally firm, settled and unequivocal. It doesn't seem to be, and in my opinion, it's no worse or better for that. (I, 12)

The idea that a shared experience is something like a 'quicksand', however, did not properly materialize in his plays until recently. (What takes place on Pinter's stage is not necessarily a direct transfer of what is taking place in his mind, it would seem.) There is a clearly traceable line in his plays of late, from 'Night' through to his most recent work *Other Places*, where 'truth' and the 'past' is considered to be what each of the storytellers wants – or fears – it to be. It is in this light that *The Collection* appears to be not only a seminal text, but the most radically sceptical of all Pinter's works, since here, as we noticed earlier, even mirrors, those faithful duplicators of reality, tend to prove 'deceptive' (II, 146).

*

By sinking into the quicksand of a multitude of confused 'realities', *The Collection* can also be seen to be the most Pirandellian of Pinter's works. Comparisons are often made, but, unlike Pinter, Pirandello was never embarrassed by overt ideological statements and never allowed himself any discrepancy – or tergiversation – between what he thought and what he wrote. For him, the two are in fact indistinguishable, the writing being an extension of his ideas. In other words, Pirandello could never afford to be an ironist like Pinter. He was ironic neither in his own idiosyncratic use of the word nor in the broader modern acceptation. In his essay entitled

'Humour', Pirandello considered irony as either a form of sarcasm or the author's awareness of the unreality of his own creations. Irony is more often used, though, in modern parlance, to indicate a sort of question mark that delicately hangs in between the utterer and the utterance, the writer and the written word. Pirandello is always obsessively in control of what he says, as if he were frightened that the words, once let loose, would take on some awful significance or would turn against their lord and master. At his most liberal, he might allow a single character to express a contrary opinion, but eventually out would come the authorial mouthpiece who would immediately set everything straight by righting all logical, emotional and conceptual wrongs uttered by the false prophet. This is the voice of truth which, paradoxically, is for ever expressing doubts about the legitimacy of truth. These authorial spokesmen, like the ghastly Laudisi in *Right You Are (If You Think You Are)*, are not the *raisonneurs* of a seventeenth-century comedy, the rationalists of a George Bernard Shaw dramatic tract, the dreadful logician figures so often derided by Ionesco, the detective inspectors ridiculed in Orton and Stoppard. They are actually the *ir*rationalists, the supposed harbingers of the Absurd, who by their very insistence prove as tedious and tiresome as their opponents. Even though Pirandello broke away from the outmoded positivist search for a single truth, he pursued just as singlemindedly the opposite view that the only truth that there is, is that there is no such thing. He preached his gospel of indeterminacy, therefore, with a blind determinist fervour.

Pinter, of course, has the advantage of the intervening sixty years of sceptical, post-Einsteinian thought on relativity which separate him from his predecessor. Despite this, *The Collection* is still often compared with Pirandello's *Right You Are (If You Think You Are)*, and critics have been wont to point out the many similarities between the two.[78] In the Italian play there is a Signor Ponza who claims that his first wife is dead and that the deceased spouse's mother, a Signora Frola, has deluded herself into believing that she is still alive and lives with Signor Ponza. Signora Frola, on the other hand, believes that Signor Ponza has deluded himself into thinking that he is a widower who has remarried; she maintains that he is in fact still living with her daughter, his first wife. When, in the final scene, Signor Ponza's first or second wife is asked to reveal the truth, she answers: 'The truth? It's only this: that I am Signora Frola's daughter and Signor Ponza's second wife.[. . .] For me, I am no one! no one! I am she whom they want me to be', which is the QED of scepticism. In *The Collection*, James's wife, Stella, claims that, when in Leeds for a fashion collection, she yielded to Bill's aggressive advances and spent the night with him; she then confesses to Harry, Bill's mature lover, that the affair was all an invention of James's own jealous fantasy. Bill first denies knowing Stella; then claims to have been seduced by her; subsequently reverts to his pristine denial; and finally admits that they did it but merely in words, talking in the lounge of the hotel 'about what we would do . . . if we did get to her room . . .' (II, 156–7). When James asks his wife whether it was true that nothing went on beyond the sexual fantasy in the lounge she 'looks at him, neither confirming nor denying' (II, 157).

The parallel between the two plays is evident, but Pirandello is far too anxious to prove his point, whereas for Pinter the 'point', if any, ought to be made obliquely, without strenuous underlining. Pinter has no need to broadcast any message concerning a relativistic creed; he is content to exploit all the dramatic tensions that such multiple ambiguities can provide. The play, which in our view is one of Pinter's very best, is a study in reciprocal misunderstanding. The young married couple and the homosexual pair seem to be able to cohabit without in the least understanding each other (which is not unlike Shakespeare, who pays the most exalted lip-service to the marriage of true minds but in fact thrives best in his portrayal of unlike spirits – think not only of *Othello* but of that incredible *ronde* of misjudgements that closes the circle of *Measure for Measure*). The only thing that is universally understood and detected is weakness – which is why Bill, the soft-centred 'slum slug' (II, 155), is bullied and wounded by James, and abused by Harry. All the characters in Pinter's plays have this psychic ability to seek out each other's weak points, but it is a power of divination which serves only to identify the slug in order to squash it without mercy.

7

MEMORY GAMES: 'OLD TIMES', 'NO MAN'S LAND' AND 'BETRAYAL'

The Collection ends, as it began, in a 'half light' which clearly suggests the haze of doubt still clouding the minds of both characters and audience. *Old Times* also begins in haze, except that here the 'dim light' suggests what he calls the 'mistiness of the past',[79] the smokescreen of time which gets in the eyes of all three of its characters. The problem of time and the mystery of the past have always played a role in Pinter's theatre. In the earliest plays, the supposed security of a present shelter (Rose's room protecting her from the outside world in *The Room*, or Stanley's lodgings keeping unwelcome guests at bay in *The Birthday Party*) is often disturbed by a menacing figure who threatens the characters with what appears to be a guilty secret, imagined or real, hidden in things that they have long forgotten. The audience is made to feel, as Harold Hobson remarked, that 'there is something in your past . . . which will catch up with you'.[80] These ghosts haunting the present rise up from both sides of the barrier of naturalism, in Ibsen as well as in Pinter.

In later plays such as *The Homecoming*, however, the roles of past and present are partly reversed. Sam's revelation of Jessie's ancient adultery does not alter the situation. It is now the present which provides the menace, whereas the past is in part the temporary refuge, as evidenced by Max's sickly reminiscences of his family life. That Max carefully embroiders upon these 'memories' to make them seem more acceptable in nostalgic retrospect is obvious, for, when he claims to remember how he was dandled and wiped and patted on the bum by his father, there is another of those pointed blackouts on the stage which serves to discredit the process of memory (III, 35). Max can no more find haven in his manufactured past than Rose and Stanley can in the speciousness of their present. The future offers no entry into an escapist world, the past no exit from the present gloom. In this sense Davies in *The Caretaker* is the wisest of all Pinter's characters: he avoids dreaming (about his future) or reminiscing (about his birthplace or country of origin). Most of the other characters, however, remain committed backward-lookers; few of them can resist Orpheus' quick look behind. There is clearly nothing to look forward to in a future, which Pinter admits 'is simply going to be the same thing. It'll never end.'[81] And so they look over their shoulders, groping back into the mistiness of their pasts to see whether some fixed point of reference can be found. After all, in line with Len's philosophical musings in *The Dwarfs*, are we *really* the same people that we were five years – or even five minutes – ago ('What you are, or appear to be to me, or appear to be to you, changes so quickly, so horrifyingly'; II, 112)? Pinter had already emphasized in 1962 'the immense difficulty, if not the impossibility, of verifying the past' (I, 11), and ten years later, in his revealing *New York Times* interview with Mel Gussow, Pinter admitted that 'the whole question of time . . . does seem to absorb me more and more'.[82] Time is created as we remember the past; it disappears as we forget it.

In Pinter, memories can be extremely short.[83] Meg is unable to reconstruct Stanley's laborious version of his aborted concert at Lower Edmonton twenty minutes after hearing the story (in *The Birthday Party*); in the final scene she remembers the disastrous party of the night before as being a lovely occasion full of dancing and singing. In other plays, however, memories can be extremely long: in *Old Times*, with its twenty years' lapse; and in *No Man's Land*, where two elderly gentlemen *seem* to evoke reminiscences from their youth. In these later plays, Pinter's view of the past appears to undergo a significant change. Time is no longer to be regarded on a linear scale, hanging down in the well of the past from whose dark bottom ghosts occasionally emerge, but on a continuum, where past and present seem to occur simultaneously. The flux is lacking. This is not unlike the circular past, free from a sequential order, of some primitive populations, which forms the basis of their mode of thinking *historically*. In our society, history is still a Christian invention, marking the great divide between what happened before the Resurrection and what happened afterwards, and making that date the turning-point in the evolution towards the City of God. But Pinter's characters are definitely not Christian. They have no future, and the past provides them with no salvation. Yet their past history often weighs them down with memories they try alternately to recapture or to obliterate. In the memory plays, characters do not evolve from their past beings; they cohabit with them. A pointer to this is the abrupt change of tense at the end of the first act of *Old Times*, as Anna and Kate revert to the *present* tense when talking of their *past* friends Charley and Jake. Another sign of temporal stasis is Hirst's key lament in *No Man's Land*, later repeated by Spooner: 'No man's land . . . does not move . . . or change . . . or grow old . . . remains . . . forever . . . icy . . . silent' (IV, 96). In these plays, the present seems to be the sum of all previous events, and the characters are consequently obliged to live in an atemporal halfway house, unable to move forward or backward, 'sitting here forever' (IV, 152), as Foster puts it.[84]

This notion of past affecting present, and present being in effect past, appears to have emerged from Pinter's close study of Proust. In 1972 he spent the entire year writing an as yet unfilmed screenplay of Proust's *A la recherche du temps perdu* with its internal awareness of time as an indivisible continuum of past and present. Pinter's *recherche* into the Proustian *recherche* seems to have encouraged the playwright towards the Bergsonian concept of *durée* (with its compelling syllogism: 'reality is change, change is indivisible, and in an indivisible change the past is one with the present'[85]). To convey Bergson's sense of 'lived time' in the theatre (*la durée vécue*), Pinter often resorts to certain cinematic and televisual devices such as flashbacks and fade-ins, devices that he became accustomed to using through writing screenplays and plays made specially for television.

Old Times (1970) opens with a particularly fine example of one such cinematic device. The stage is at first shrouded in a 'dim light', with the lights gradually brightening to reveal Anna lurking mysteriously in the shadows, while Kate and Deeley, the husband and wife, talk quietly about her in the foreground.[86] Anna, it transpires, was once Kate's flatmate in London, but the more Kate strains to remember her old friend, the more the 'mistiness' of her past becomes evident. The play starts *in media verba*, if we may coin the expression, since its first word, 'Dark', is Kate's answer to a question from Deeley that the audience is not allowed to hear. As they talk about their absent guest, there seems to be a sudden flashback in time as Anna herself dramatically materializes from out of their shadowy past – becomes physically and alertly *present* in the room – the literal embodiment of old times gone by spent among the 'arty' cafés of post-war London (just as Madame Pace is evoked and summoned on the stage by the painful memories of the Father in Pirandello's *Six Characters in Search of an Author*). This piece of theatrical wizardry has the effect of immediately conveying a sense of synchronic – rather than diachronic – time, since, from the outset, past and present are both manifest on the stage simultaneously, though with a different status (light versus dark; centre of the room versus window; foreground versus background).

But Anna is both a ghost from the past and an old friend come to stay. She represents for Kate a sentimentalized view of her past, while Deeley, her husband, represents for her the 'brutish' sensuality of the ever-present. The play describes Anna's and Deeley's strenuous efforts to gain possession of Kate. In allegorical terms, this seems a struggle between Time Past and Time Present. But in Pinter, unlike in T. S. Eliot, there is no 'time future contained in time past'.[87] *Old Times* is definitely not the first instalment of a serial; nor is *No Man's Land*. The characters from these plays are cut off from their future by their unchristian despair. In *Old Times* the battle-ground is the past, and the competition between Anna and

Deeley is centred around two 'remembered' anecdotes, the first concerning the film *Odd Man Out*, the second the Wayfarers Tavern 'off the Brompton Road'. Deeley 'remembers' both incidents as peculiarly squalid affairs now best forgotten, but Anna's memories are fonder, in accordance with her eulogizing the past as some sort of improbable paradise lost. Both have resorted to playing a watchful game of 'consequences', and the (nonsensical) difference between their two stories is best seen in juxtaposition. Here, for instance, are their greatly varying accounts of the day both claim they went to see *Odd Man Out*:

DEELEY. [. . .] Some bloody awful summer afternoon, walking in no direction. I remember thinking there was something familiar about the neighbourhood[. . . .] and there was this fleapit showing Odd Man Out and there were two usherettes standing in the foyer and one of them was stroking her breasts and the other one was saying 'dirty bitch' [. . .]. And there was only one other person in the cinema . . . and there she [i.e. Kate] is. (IV, 25–6)

ANNA. [. . .] I remember one Sunday she [i.e. Kate] said to me, looking up from the paper, come quick, quick, come with me quickly, and we seized our handbags and went, on a bus, to some totally obscure, some totally unfamiliar district and, almost alone, saw a wonderful film called Odd Man Out. (IV, 34)

Everything about these two accounts seems to differ. Deeley remembers walking aimlessly in an area known to him, Anna remembers travelling purposely by bus to a 'totally unfamiliar district'. More significantly, both remember seeing Kate in the cinema, but neither acknowledges the presence of the other (though Anna may have been one of the usherettes and Deeley is not altogether excluded by Anna's reminiscence, since she states only that she and Kate were 'almost alone'). It becomes clear during the course of the play that Deeley and Anna both remember the same incident very differently. As Anna states in her crucial remark: 'There are things I remember which may never have happened but as I recall them so they take place' (IV, 28).[88] The idea of creating one's past independently of chronicle and history, so to speak, is very close to the world of Penelope Mortimer's *The Pumpkin Eater* (a novel for which Pinter has written a screenplay), which concludes with the following passage: 'Some of these things happened, and some were dreams. They are all true, as I understood truth. They are all real, as I understood reality.' The same applies to the incident in the Wayfarers Tavern (or is it the party at Westbourne Grove?), where it is never made entirely clear whether it was Anna's skirt or Kate's that Deeley spent a whole evening 'gazing' up. Nor can one categorically say – despite the many teasing allusions to it – that Kate was or was not involved in a lesbian relationship with Anna. They might have been, of course, but, because of the 'immense difficulty' in 'verifying the past', it is never conclusively established – frustratingly for Deeley. (Similarly, no matter how hard Marcel, the narrator in Proust's novel, tries to get at the truth, he can never be entirely sure whether his lover Albertine has been having a lesbian affair with her great friend Andrée or not.)

*

In *No Man's Land* (1974), Pinter's next major play, it is just as impossible to distinguish between genuine reminiscences, memories modified by the process of time, and recollections stultified for strategic purposes. They all seem to have equal weight in the confident aggressiveness of Spooner's irony (who is surely the greatest ironic character in the English theatre since Shakespeare). Spooner, a 'man in his sixties', is an outsider seeking, after the fashion of Davies in *The Caretaker* and Ruth in *The Homecoming*, to ingratiate himself into the apparent sanctuary of an established household (in this respect, but in few others, *No Man's Land* represents a backward step in the direction of the early 'two people in a room' plays). The household in this case is overseen by Hirst, an elderly alcoholic and, supposedly, a well-known man of letters, who seems to have been at one time a university acquaintance of Spooner's. If appearances are not deceptive, Hirst happens to have had more success in his chosen career as a writer than the tramp-like Spooner, who claims to be a fellow poet but collects glasses in a pub and is very shabbily dressed. Hirst remains, in stark contrast, 'precisely dressed' throughout, and his assured status in society is reinforced by the physical, flanking presence of his two wards (keepers?), Foster and Briggs, who are constantly at his side, eyeing the sudden intrusion of Spooner with deep suspicion.

The play begins with two opening gambits which in their own way are every bit as remarkable as the cinematic entrance in *Old Times*. By definition the *incipit* must be shocking and alienating, since it forces us to enter into a dark room, without knowing what or whom to expect there. Nothing can rival the intimate aggression of the first line of a text which lures the reader into a territory whose conventions, location, rules, time-scale and habits are unknown. 'Who's there?' 'Nay, answer me; stand and unfold yourself' is no mean example of initial shock (from *Hamlet*). Pinter is a master of the opening strategy (when the author tries to defeat the reader or the spectator on the chess-board of the text). We have already noted the powerful impact of *The Birthday Party*'s first few lines. *No Man's Land* begins just as devastatingly:

HIRST. As it is?
SPOONER. As it is, yes please, absolutely as it is.

Hirst's demand is an immediate throwing down of the gauntlet, and the exact phrasing of Spooner's rejoinder suggests a commitment on his part to tell the truth, the whole truth and nothing but the truth (a commitment which, needless to say, is soon broken). Hirst and Spooner attempt to control each other through a manipulation of the past, which is either unknowable or modifiable at will. The rich and the poor, the successful writer and the unsuccessful poet, the parched dipsomaniac and the thirsty beggar, fight for two hours, creating and destroying plausible and implausible backgrounds, inventing different versions of the past in which they had met or not met; known or not known each other; seduced or not seduced their respective wives or women friends. The factual truth of these

89

fanciful reconstructions is demoted, since what seems to matter is the game of pressures and counter-pressures. The recollection or invention of a second wife, of a different mistress, of a new experience, of a different lifestyle, of different war years (Hirst: 'You did say you had a good war, didn't you?' Spooner: 'A rather good one, yes'; IV, 129), are gambits in the social game. Autobiography becomes subservient to the necessity of survival, to the requirements of polemics. The character has been married, or fought a war, or belonged to a club, or turned into a homosexual or a voyeur, if this item of information can be used to humiliate the opponent.

The initial sparring encounter is cut short by Hirst's drink-sodden departure on Briggs's arm, but it starts up again the very moment that Hirst reappears in the second act, when he issues a fresh challenge to Spooner by addressing him, with apparent friendliness, as 'Charles'. It is tempting to say that Spooner *decides* to take up this challenge by tentatively assuming the new persona that has been offered him, but the play does not provide sufficient evidence to let us *decide* whether Spooner *decided* anything. 'Temperamentally I can be what you wish' (IV, 147), says Spooner the chameleon to Hirst. In fact, he can modify not only his temperament but his name, identity, social position, past experience, residence, identity, war record, and so on and so forth – because, side by side with the battle of memory, *No Man's Land* records Spooner's need to settle down, which makes him available to any moral, social or sexual prostitution that will solve his problem. But the density and pungency of the dialogue distract us from the drama of the two men (destitution and squalor for Spooner; for Hirst 'the last lap of a race . . . [he] had long forgotten to run'; IV, 94), and focuses on the brilliance of the verbal duel rather than on the revelations of anguish and despair. The play is a compromise between the linguistic idiosyncrasies of the characters (especially in the case of Spooner, the aged bohemian whose speech is an exquisite florilegium of revolting clichés) and their personal drama built on psychological emptiness. Spooner and Hirst are linguistic shells made of words words words, but there is nothing inside, since a man with two lives has no life of his own; a man with several pasts has no past that belongs to him.

The characters in *Old Times* enter a sort of time-machine; Hirst and Spooner in *No Man's Land* enter a sort of brain-machine, modifying the links connecting stored recollections and convenient memories. Their past, rather than recollected, is created anew – or should we say askew? – from the imaginative perspective of the present. Pinter has said in this respect that the past is not only what you remember; it is also what you 'imagine you remember, convince yourself you remember, or pretend to remember'.[89] The verbs *remember*, *imagine*, *convince* and *pretend* cover all possibilities: memory, oblivion, anamnesis, intentional and unintentional distortions, buried recollections, lies and bloody lies.

The *creative* recollections of Spooner and Hirst are much akin to those remembered by Justices Shallow and Silence in *Henry IV, Part 2*. Both pairs in the ancient and in the modern play are old, and claim to remember their wild youths spent respectively at the Inns of Court and at Oxford. They all remember hearing the 'chimes of midnight' with such fictional ladies as Jane Nightwork and Stella Winstanley, and recall their old drinking friends, now dead (Shallow speaks of the 'mad days that I have spent! And to see how many of my old acquaintance are dead!', which is echoed by Hirst: 'What a bunch. What a night, as I recall. All dead now, of course'; IV, 127). Spooner at first mirrors Silence in his quiet acceptance of his passive, listening role; but when Hirst begins to brag about being 'successful awfully early' (IV, 128) Spooner launches into an attack on his antagonist's past, just as Falstaff abuses Shallow's hospitality in his great soliloquy beginning 'Lord, Lord, how subject we old men are to this vice of lying!' (III, ii). Like Anna with Deeley in *Old Times*, Spooner can always counter a particular remembrance with his own different remembrance of the same event, which his opponent has to accept as being equally valid. Since the real past is for ever lost to human memory (or perhaps it is this 'real' past which is the bogus concept), we have to make do with an ersatz past, as Pinter intimated in his interview with Gussow: 'The fact is it's terribly difficult to define what happened at any time. . . . So much is imagined and that imagining is as true as real.'[90]

*

In *Betrayal* (1978), his most recent full-length play, and his most commercially successful in the USA, Pinter covers the same linguistic material as in the two previous plays, *Old Times* and *No Man's Land*. In his early work Pinter had proved to be an artist of mimicry, aping the inarticulacy and conceptual confusion of everyday speech. In the later plays, however, all this is gone. Characters have become articulate, intelligent, cultivated, literate, with no speech impediment, glottal stop or mental occlusion. Yet they are still able to articulate the dead weight of small talk – of microscopic talk – which Pinter orchestrates in virtuoso fashion. Pinter can revive glimmers of significance in the most unpromising areas of speech. In his dialogues, the barter of clichés, the exchange of casual remarks, the tit-for-tat of gossip and futile observations, are raised to the realm of dramatic art. Tittle-tattle is rescued by Pinter from its conceptual void and elevated to an important role in the social strategy, for both a moron like Gus in *The Dumb Waiter* and a sophisticated man like Robert in *Betrayal*.

Betrayal is also close to *Old Times* in its basic conflict: a plot that 'revolves around the conventional triangle', as one critic puts it,[91] with two competitors striving for control over a third (Emma, the wife and clandestine lover). Or is it? Although the author anticipated any criticism about repetition with his self-indulgent pun in the first scene, 'Just like *old times*' (IV, 158; our italics), *Betrayal* does not really concern itself with the vicious triangulation of love. The play, of course, breaks new ground in a rather spectacular fashion by going backward rather than forward (and in this Pinter may have been inspired by similar experiments with a partly inverted chronology in Beckett's *Krapp's Last Tape* and Stoppard's *Artist Descending a Staircase*). It progresses and regresses along the lines of an adulterous affair between Jerry and Emma: from the aftermath of the breakdown, back to the tired final phase, then to its climax, right down to its ebullient beginning. It regresses in time, but it progresses from apathy to passion – well, almost passion. It is like a Spanish game, *el juego del reves*. A group of children stands in a circle with the king in the middle, who says a word – for example, *caracol* – which must be answered in a split second by the children with the same word, only in reverse order of letters – *locarac*. The game is an apt metaphor for many experiments in modern art which seek to explore the dark side of the moon. Pinter too is an astronaut of the unlit hemisphere,[92] denouncing the fragility of our concepts of cause and effect in his journey back through time.

Of course, the idea of reversing time in a play is a gimmick, a con-trick, like an ice-skater going backwards to show off their skill. But it is a gimmick that works, not only dramatically but conceptually. The reverse gear helps us to understand not the characters but rather our own incompetence. As we try to link different episodes in life by means of cause and effect, and effect and cause, we come to realize that the whole concept of causality is fictitious (a gigantic con-trick by the historians?). Divination is bogus, but backward divination (also called history) is bunk. The very idea of history is thereby devalued, since cause does not follow effect in this backward journey. By focusing on the behaviour of three people down the pit of time, we discover that all events are discrete (following Popper's idea about the 'poverty of historicism'). A knowledge of the political, economical and ideological situation in Paris in the 1880s obviously does not help us to foresee what happened there in the 1890s, unless we have read the right books or consulted the proper sources; but neither does it help us to understand what happened in the 1870s. The historians – and the futurologists – are the real con-men.[93]

Audiences have often complained that Pinter has not provided any background information about his characters. Who are they? Where did they come from? Which school were they at? Whom did they bank with? These complaints have proved groundless, since Pinter is now providing information by unfolding the past events scene by scene, the result being that we are none the wiser. *Betrayal* is a desperate play for spectators, who ought to learn from it the feebleness of their claims to knowledge. *Betrayal* is also a desperate play for a different reason: the characters do not deserve to be so empty. Aimed at an upper-middle-class audience who can identify with the three characters, the play is more persuasive on a social level than the previous ones, because there is less distance between characters and spectators. If we list the heroes and heroines in Pinter, we find that most of them are desperate because of a pang of guilt or a twist of fate. Something went wrong with their lives, from Stanley in *The Birthday Party* to Hirst in *No Man's Land*. But nothing is wrong with Robert, Emma and Jerry; and, what is worse, nothing goes wrong with them. Like the characters in Simon Gray's *Butley* and *Otherwise Engaged* (which Pinter directed in their opening London productions), they are intelligent, articulate, cultivated people, free and responsible, open-minded and well adjusted, engaged in interesting activities. They can choose of their own free will where their allegiances lie and what they want to make of their own lives, which are by no means tragic. Yet Pinter has succeeded in conveying a feeling of immense desolation. 'I don't think we don't love each other' is Jerry's pusillanimous claim to Emma (with its beautiful double-negative; IV, 197). Emma's new lover, Casey, is 'Writing a novel about a man who leaves his wife and three children and goes to live alone on the other side of London to write a novel about a man who leaves his wife and three children' (IV, 206). And then there is Robert's remark to his wife about his squash partner, Jerry: 'I've always liked Jerry. To be honest, I've always liked him rather more than I've liked you. Maybe I should have had an affair with him myself' (IV, 225), which is not a homosexual confession (?), but the proof that squash is stronger than love.

8

DIFFERENT BALL GAMES:
'THE FRENCH LIEUTENANT'S WOMAN'
AND 'OTHER PLACES'

In his interview with Mel Gussow, Pinter was asked what he did after *The Homecoming*, at a time when he felt he could no longer write another stage play. This was his reply: 'I kept busy one way or the other. Films, I suppose. It's not quite the same thing as something really coming out from the bottom of your spine.'[94] Even in the 'minor' art of writing screenplays, where Pinter has yet to find a highly individualized style, a suitable expression for his own dramatic genius, he has still managed to show a phenomenal technical ability (not unlike his skill as a stage craftsman) and an exceptional capacity for narrative concentration. This can easily be confirmed by browsing through his magnificent script for Proust's *A la recherche du temps perdu* (still waiting for a producer), the celebrated trilogy of scripts he wrote for Joseph Losey in the 1960s, and now the recently published screenplay of *The French Lieutenant's Woman*, based on the novel by John Fowles, which was filmed in the summer of 1980. Since the earlier scripts have been widely reviewed, both from the point of view of adaptation and as cinema, we shall concentrate on this latest piece, which so far has not been fully analysed.

To adapt a novel of ideas for the cinema is a formidable task. On the one hand is the novelist who, in Fowles's own words, is 'addicted to the solitary freedoms of prose fiction', a lofty creator who wants to play 'producer, director, all the cast *and* camera' (p. x). On the other hand there is, ideally, a sort of machine: a *transformer*, who acts as both filter and condenser, recycling all the ideas, emotions, mechanisms, mannerisms, passions, desires, *trouvailles*, digressions and tricks of the original text, hoping to siphon them off into a hopelessly small container. The limitations of the medium impose severe restrictions on the scriptwriter's scope. A film is usually not more than 120 minutes in length, and the script comprises perhaps 250 short visual-literary paragraphs, no more than a few lines each, which are meant to be the screen equivalent for hundreds of pages of dense prose. The result is often a text replete with non-dramatic dialogue. This is not necessarily the fault of the scriptwriter, but of the material itself, which refuses to be translated from one genre to the other (especially when it is supposed to contain 'ideas').

This is particularly true of *The French Lieutenant's Woman*, a Victorian narrative commented upon by a contemporary voice which is itself located inside the novel. Prospective film producers were drawn by the original format of Fowles's novel, with its hybrid mixture of novel and meta-novel, historical narrative and meta-historical commentary. They were 'profoundly uninterested in buying a latterday Victorian romance when there were hundreds of the genuine article . . . lying about out of copyright and to be had for nothing', as Fowles jokingly claims in his Foreword to Pinter's published script (p. xi). The *transformer*, in short, was being asked to adapt two distinct but overlapping texts: the love story between Charles Smithson and Sarah Woodruff, and the musings of the modern narrator on the margin of that story.

According to Fowles, Pinter has succeeded – where others had notably failed – in writing a 'brilliant metaphor' for the original novel (p. xii). The film opts for two quite radical solutions to the problem of the novel's 'stereoscopic vision' (p. x): the transformation from narrator's comment to actor's voice, and the metamorphosis of Sarah from a person sensitive to art to the very artist herself (whether these were Pinter's own decisions, or whether he took them in consultation with his director, Karel Reisz, is not clear).[95]

Up to a point, the first solution works. The film multiplies the visual and conceptual angles of the love story, and shows us the hero and heroine both in the dramatic interpretations of the actors and in the comments that these actors make as they prepare to enter their roles. Instead of having Fowles tell us (a) that Sarah smiled when she saw the two young lovers, Mary and Sam, in the wood; (b) what Charles thought of that smile; (c) what the narrator thought of Charles's thought, Pinter sets an opposition between, say, Sarah stumbling in the under-growth and Anna (the actress who is supposed to act the part of the French Lieutenant's woman) attempting to understand what is the meaning of that stumbling – strategically, psycholo-gically, emotionally – in one of the most beautiful scenes in the film (pp. 29–30). Where the script does not seem to work is in the modern love story between Anna (Sarah) and Mike (who is meant to play the role of Charles). Here, inevitably, the melo-dramatic impetus of the original story, the Victorian love-affair, so forcefully opposed and slow to come to life, is much more fascinating than the modern one, which appears facile and uncommitted. Every time the film moves to the modern love-scenes, the audience hopes that they will soon be over so that they will get back to Charles and Sarah's fate.

The second transformation also poses problems. Sarah is no longer the inspirer of the Pre-Raphaelite Brotherhood, as in the novel: she has herself become the artist – a draughtsman and perhaps painter of great talent who has discovered the courage to face her own career as an artist in the culminating moment of her life as a seducing or seduced 'whore' (see Chapter 5). Unfortunately, the creative side of Sarah has been inadequately developed. The film, especially in the interpretation of Meryl Streep, gives us teasing insights into the complex mechanisms of Sarah's emotions and wants, but it offers no suggestion that the protagonist is endowed with an artistic nature. To put it bluntly, we spectators can understand why it would be worth it for Charles to sacrifice his life, reputation and career in order to become, even for a short night, the prey or predator of that woman; but not to spend one hundred dollars to buy one of her drawings, simply because their creative inspiration has not been sufficiently presented.

These criticisms aside, Pinter seems to us extraordinarily

skilful at forshortening, into a single image or brief utterance, the social and psychological intricacies that Fowles develops at great length in the novel. (We would endorse Fowles's generous assessment that Pinter has a 'truly remarkable gift for reducing the long and complex without distortion'; p. xi). The mutual and stubborn incomprehension between master and servant, which preoccupies the novelist who is ever sensitive to class relations, and Charles's inadequacy in trying to understand Sam's ways of thinking and feeling, is luminously condensed into one shot (Charles with a telescope looking at Sam who courts a girl near a flower-stall) and a solitary sentence ('When we get there be sure you don't dally with Miss Ernestina's maid'; pp. 2–3). Similarly, aspects of Charles's betrothed are obliquely but succinctly conveyed by Mary, the maid, commenting about the impossibility of Ernestina's refusing Charles: 'Never. She'd give her left arm. *And* all her dresses' (p. 7). The novel's lengthy description of metropolitan prostitution is solved in the film by a rapid reckoning from Mike, who calculates the statistical data about Victorian London and comes to the conclusion: 'Outside marriage, a Victorian gentleman had about two point four fucks a week' (p. 19). The double ending of the novel is sublimated by the remarkable shot of the rowing boat entering on to a sunny lake (with Sarah sitting in the prow and Charles by the oars) and by the displacement from Chelsea to Windermere (another location associated with artistic bohemianism) – though given the pragmatics of film production perhaps there were rather more prosaic reasons for this change of setting.

*

Another area in which Pinter has always been very active is radio. *A Slight Ache*, *A Night Out* and *The Dwarfs* all appeared first on the radio, along with a number of revue sketches written in 1964, often especially commissioned for the Third Programme in London by the then head of BBC radio drama, Martin Esslin. *Landscape* too was first broadcast on the radio when it encountered serious censorship problems on the stage. But it is his latest short play for the radio, *Family Voices* (also broadcast by the BBC, in January 1981), which is perhaps his highest achievement to date in the medium. Like Beckett, Pinter has adapted himself to this medium with apparent relative ease, since his style has always shown a tendency towards the purely verbal effects of the radio.

In *Family Voices* there is no communion or choric harmony, only a cacophonic division of voices which seems to operate on three separate wavelengths. There is a mother, a father and a son, who pretend to write letters which perhaps have never been posted, but only thought out. Reality, as so often in Pinter, is at least double: the father is dead or alive; the mother, abandoned by her son, tenderly complains about his absence, or alternatively curses him for his indifference ('I wait for your letter begging me to come to you. I'll spit on it'; IV, 290); she defends him from calumnies, or denounces him to the police. The son, for his part, is happy in the anonymity of the metropolis, or desperately unhappy; he seduces the landlady's niece, or is seduced by an old pederast; he lives in an aristocratic home, or a house of ill repute. Only a few things seem certain: the story is disturbing; the characters are inhuman; affections are untrustworthy; hostilities are genuine; benevolence is deceitful; malevolence is triumphant.

Family Voices has now been reprinted together with two new short plays, *Victoria Station* and *A Kind of Alaska*, in a volume entitled *Other Places*. The three plays were staged at the National Theatre, London, in October 1982 under the direction of Peter Hall. *Victoria Station* is a comic sketch, much in the manner of Pinter's earlier attempts at the genre (from *Trouble in the Works* to *Last to Go*), but on a wider scale. It is a dialogue over the radio between the controller of a minicab company and an absent-minded driver, who is apparently stuck outside Crystal Palace in the middle of the night and refuses to go anywhere, not even to a station called Victoria which he has never heard of. He is lost in the night of London and in the yet foggier night of his own brain. He wants to stay put because, he claims, he has a female passenger in the back with whom he has fallen in love. But the audience cannot see her: she might be a figment of his imagination, or perhaps he has killed her and kept the body on the back seat. The play, in typical Pinterian fashion, refuses to be more explicit.

But the real novelty of this new volume is in the third play, *A Kind of Alaska*, which seems to mark a turning-point in Pinter's theatrical interests. It draws its material from *Awakenings*, a haunting book by Oliver Sacks, physician by profession and writer by vocation, which had considerable echo even in the literary world when it first appeared.[96] In the late sixties, Sacks started to administer L-DOPA, a new drug against Parkinsonism, to patients suffering from sleeping sickness (*encephalitis lethargica*). Several were thus *awakened* from a long sleep which in some cases had lasted up to twenty or thirty years. *Awakenings* is not a miracle story, but the reporting of a day-by-day fight against a disease that can be counter-attacked but never defeated. Sacks surveys twenty clinical cases and dramatizes (in the noblest sense) the alternate course of the cure. Every gram added or subtracted in the daily injection of L-DOPA has enormous repercussions on the physical and psychical state of the patient. Symptoms chase each other in a diabolic roundabout: any improvement in a given area of human behaviour can have terrifying side-effects in a different, sometimes unforeseeable, area. *Awakenings* relates this Herculean fight against the hydra – the monster which grows several heads for each one that is cut off – in a series of clinical studies which are among the most moving of modern literature.

Pinter tells the story of Deborah (based on the real case of Rose R.) and her awakening after the first injection of L-DOPA from a lethargic state which had lasted twenty-nine years. Deborah fell asleep when she was sixteen and comes back to life at forty-five, a traveller without luggage, caught between her ontological and her official age, between her adolescent fantasies and her adult body. The play presents some similarities with Pirandello's *Enrico Quarto*, which concerns a twentieth-century man, convinced that he is Henry IV, the twelfth-century German emperor, who spends several decades of his life exiled in the dreamland of his own fantasies. But Pinter avoids the cumbersome melodramatic structure of Pirandello's tale and allows only the emotional content of Deborah's story to filter through the icy linearity and atrocious simplicity of his own language. During the twenty-nine years of her long night, Deborah has been far, very far away, in a kind of Alaska; and the ballast of her personal memories, which she carries inside her now ageless body, includes unknown materials, minerals not included in Mendeleyev's table brought back to earth by an extragalactic probe. We have therefore two simultaneous dramas: the Pirandellian drama of the great yawning gap at the very centre of Deborah's life; and the existential drama created by the confrontation with the unknown, with the documentary reportage about life in the distant planet of nothingness. Pinter does not play on the fairy-tale element and refuses to grant the patient the magical status of a Sleeping Beauty, immune to the biological laws which regulate the ageing process. Deborah's only mythical dimension is in the long experience of lethargic absence.

But even this reading of ours of the last short plays seems presumptuous; indeed, *all* of our readings of Pinter's plays have seemed presumptuous to a degree. Pinter, like his characters, is a master of mimicry, a Houdini of the text. Though he has denied being the kind of uncommitted writer who refuses to take responsibility for his work,[97] he remains practised at the art of disengaging himself from the tiresome responsibility of authorship, whereby author and text overlap, the one being the blueprint for the other. Pinter cannot be pinned down to any view expressed by a character or extracted from his plays by a critic's dental pliers. He is like Macavity, the Napoleon of crime in T. S. Eliot's ironic poem, 'Macavity: The Mystery Cat': 'when they reach the scene of crime, *Macavity's not there*'. Though his words linger around the venue of many a scandalous verbal outrage, Harold Pinter is *not there*.

NOTES

1 The title of an early article by Richard Schechner, *Tulane Drama Review*, 11 (Winter 1966), pp. 176–84.

2 For a more comprehensive analysis of Pinter's 'idiom of lies', see Guido Almansi, 'Harold Pinter's Idiom of Lies', *Contemporary English Drama*, Stratford-upon-Avon Studies 19 (1981), pp. 78–92.

3 Pinter maintains that he is 'not terribly bothered about new forms' in 'Harold Pinter Replies', interview with Harry Thompson, *New Theatre Magazine* (January 1961), p. 10.

4 Pinter shows his dislike for improvisation in 'Why Doesn't He Write More?', interview with Patricia Bosworth, *New York Times*, 27 October 1968.

5 From Charles Marowitz's Introduction to *A Macbeth: Freely Adapted from Shakespeare's Tragedy* (London, 1971).

6 Karl Kraus, *Beim Wort Genommen* (Munich, 1955), p. 14 (Kraus is referring specifically to women).

7 Oscar Wilde, Preface to *The Picture of Dorian Gray*.

8 See Roland Barthes, 'The Death of the Author', in *Image–Music–Text* (London, 1977), pp. 142–9.

9 According to Viktor Shklovsky, literary strategy follows oblique lines like the Knight move at chess.

10 We use the terms of Michel Foucault in his classic study, *Les Mots et les choses* (Paris, 1966) (English edition, *The Order of Things: An Archaeology of the Human Sciences* (London, 1970)).

11 August Strindberg, Preface to *Miss Julie*.

12 François Rabelais, Prologue to Book I of *Gargantua and Pantagruel*.

13 Pinter, reply to an open letter from Leonard Russell, *Sunday Times* (London), 14 August 1960, p. 21.

14 From an interview with Kenneth Tynan (October 1960), as

quoted in Martin Esslin, *The Theatre of the Absurd*, rev. edn (Harmondsworth, 1968), p. 274.

15 R. D. Laing, *Knots* (Harmondsworth, 1972), p. 1.

16 Pinter claims that 'we communicate only too well, in our silence, in what is unsaid, and . . . what takes place is a continual evasion, desperate rearguard attempts to keep ourselves to ourselves' (I, 15).

17 Eric Berne, *Games People Play* (Harmondsworth, 1968), p. 151. Berne is mentioned with reference to Pinter in a number of critical works; see especially Lois G. Gordon, *Stratagems to Uncover Nakedness: The Dramas of Harold Pinter* (Columbia, Mo., 1968).

18 'An Interview with Lawrence M. Bensky', repr. in C. Marowitz and S. Trussler (eds), *Theatre at Work* (London, 1967), p. 105.

19 Berne, op. cit., p. 44.

20 Ludwig Wittgenstein, *Philosophical Investigations*, trans. G. E. M. Anscombe (Oxford, 1963), p. 249.

21 See Irving Wardle, 'A Director's Approach: An Interview with Peter Hall', in John and Anthea Lahr (eds), *A Casebook on Harold Pinter's The Homecoming* (New York, 1971), p. 22.

22 Johann Huizinga, *Homo Ludens: A Study of the Play Element in Culture* (1949; London, 1970), p. 30.

23 The literary allusion is to Sir Henry Newbolt's poem, *Vitae Lampada*.

24 They have been published together, along with *The Pumpkin Eater* and *The Quiller Memorandum*, in *Five Screenplays* (London, 1971).

25 Berne, op. cit., pp. 108–9. Steven H. Gale, *Butter's Going Up: A Critical Analysis of Harold Pinter's Work* (Durham, NC, 1977), p. 127, also refers to this game in connection with *The Basement* and *The Collection*.

26 Bernard F. Dukore, *Harold Pinter*, Macmillan Master Dramatists (London and Basingstoke, 1982), pp. 72 and 84, makes much the same points with regard to ambiguous endings in *The Basement* and *The Homecoming*.

27 Roman Jakobson, 'Closing Statement: Linguistics and Poetics', in T. Sebeok (ed.), *Style and Language* (Cambridge, Mass., 1960), p. 357. See also Deirdre Burton on 'statements-as-requests-for-confirmation', 'Making Conversation: On Conversational Analysis, Stylistics, and Pinter', *Language and Style* (1979), pp. 188–200.

28 'In an Empty Bandstand – Harold Pinter in Conversation', interview with Joan Bakewell, *The Listener*, 82 (6 November 1968), pp. 630–1.

29 In T. S. Eliot's phrase, from 'The Love Song of J. Alfred Prufrock'; Hirst mentions how he used to go to sleep 'after tea and toast' in *No Man's Land* (IV, 106).

30 Martin Esslin, *Pinter: A Study of his Plays* (London, 1973), p. 205.

31 Arlene Sykes, *Harold Pinter* (Atlantic Highlands, NJ, 1970), p. 79.

32 Ibid., p. 21.

33 For an analysis of chatter in the modern theatre, see Alberto Moravia, 'The Theatre of Chatting', *London Magazine* (July–August 1969), pp. 94–109.

34 As Pinter says: 'I have mixed feelings about words. . . . Moving among them, sorting them out, watching them appear on the page, from this I derive a considerable pleasure. But at the same time I have another strong feeling about words which amounts to nothing less than nausea' (I, 13).

35 William Howard Gass, *On Being Blue: A Philosophical Inquiry* (Boston, Mass., 1976), p. 11.

36 'It's one more thing we do to the poor, the deprived: cut out their tongues . . . allow them a language as lousy as their lives' (ibid., p. 25).

37 Estragon says: 'let us try and converse calmly, since we are incapable of keeping silent.' Samuel Beckett, *Waiting for Godot* (London, 1956), p. 62.

38 *The Gentleman Dancing-Master* (1673), II, ii. Wycherley remarks: 'He is as dull as a country-squire at questions and commands'.

39 Pinter, letter to *The Times* (London), 22 March 1974, p. 17.

40 'An Interview with Lawrence M. Bensky', p. 104.

41 William Baker and Stephen Ely Tabachnick, *Harold Pinter* (Edinburgh, 1973), p. 88.

42 Roland Barthes discusses 'pensive' texts in *S/Z*, trans. R. Miller (London, 1975), pp. 216–17.

43 'An Interview with Lawrence M. Bensky', p. 103.

44 Arthur Rimbaud, letter to Georges Izambard, 13 May 1871.

45 Jacques Lacan, 'Le Séminaire sur la lettre volée', in *Ecrits*, 1 (Paris, 1966), p. 24.

46 The point is made by Arnold P. Hinchcliffe, *Harold Pinter*, Twayne's English Authors (New York, 1967), p. 88. Peter Hall talks of Pinter's characters 'taking the piss' in Lahr (eds), op. cit., p. 14.

47 Pinter has said that he is constantly dealing with characters 'at the extreme edge of their living, where they are living pretty much

alone', in an interview with Kenneth Tynan (October 1960), quoted in Esslin, *The Theatre of the Absurd*, p. 290.

48 In 'An Interview with Lawrence M. Bensky', p. 108.

49 See 'Filming *The Caretaker*', interview with Pinter and Clive Donner (the director) led by Kenneth Cavander, *Transatlantic Review*, 13 (1963), pp. 17–26.

50 Interview with Kenneth Tynan (October 1960), quoted in Esslin, *The Theatre of the Absurd*, p. 280.

51 An open seminar at the University of East Anglia, 1981. Pinter had in fact already claimed that *The Caretaker* was 'about love' in a remark quoted by Charles Marowitz in 'Theatre Abroad', *Village Voice*, 1 September 1960.

52 A remark made at a Drama Desk luncheon in New York, 9 January 1967. See 'Probing Pinter's Play', with Henry Hewes, *Saturday Review* (April 1967).

53 In 'An Interview with Lawrence M. Bensky', p. 103.

54 Ibid.

55 See Lahr (eds), op. cit., p. 14; and Peter Hall, 'Directing Pinter', *Theatre Quarterly* (1974–5), p. 6.

56 'A Director's Approach: An Interview with Peter Hall', in Lahr (eds), op. cit., pp. 21–2.

57 Respectively, Paul Rogers, as quoted in 'Probing Pinter's Play', *Saturday Review* (April 1967), p. 56; and Margaret Croydon, 'Pinter's Hideous Comedy', in Lahr (eds), op. cit., p. 50.

58 See, for instance, Lucina Paquet Gabbard, *The Dream Structure of Pinter's Plays* (Madison, NJ, 1976); and Katherine H. Burkman, *The Dramatic World of Harold Pinter: Its Basis in Ritual* (Columbus, Ohio, 1971).

59 Irving Wardle, 'The Territorial Struggle', in Lahr (eds), op. cit., pp. 37–44.

60 Dukore, op. cit., p. 84, also likens Ruth to a queen bee, 'a worker who supports the drones'.

61 See Lahr (eds), op. cit., pp. 21–2.

62 Extract from a letter written to Peter Wood, director of the first London production of *The Birthday Party* (at the Lyric Theatre), 30 March 1958. As quoted by Pinter in an open seminar at the University of East Anglia, 1981.

63 In similar vein, Pinter has also said: 'To supply an explicit moral tag to an evolving and compulsive dramatic image seems to be facile, impertinent and dishonest' (I, 12).

64 Gabbard, op. cit., p. 260; Esslin, *Pinter: A Study of his Plays*, p. 151; Nigel Alexander, 'Past, Present and Pinter', *Essays and Studies*, 27 (1974), p. 10.

65 The title of an early attempt at Pinter bibliography by Lois G. Gordon, *Theatre Documentation*, 1 (1968), pp. 3–20.

66 See, in particular, Martin Esslin, *Pinter: A Study of his Plays*, pp. 137–57, and '*The Homecoming*: An Interpretation', in Lahr (eds), op. cit., pp. 1–8.

67 Augusta Walker, 'Why the Lady Does It', in Lahr (eds), op. cit., p. 117. Her suggested answer is that 'she does it because she finds herself returned to a world that profoundly needs her and that has a strangle grip on her heart' (p. 118).

68 A. J. Ayer, *Language, Truth and Logic* (London, 1936), p. 35.

69 See note 1.

70 Anonymous review, *Manchester Guardian*, 20 May 1958.

71 In an interview with Patricia Bosworth, 'Why Doesn't He Write More?', *New York Times*, 27 October 1968.

72 Felix Barber, *Evening News* (London), 18 September 1970, p. 3.

73 In a speech given at the opening of the Samuel Beckett Exhibition, University of Reading, 19 May 1971.

74 As quoted in 'A Conversation (Pause) with Harold Pinter', interview with Mel Gussow, *New York Times Magazine*, 5 December 1971, p. 43.

75 Dukore, op. cit., p. 100.

76 As Pinter remarked in an interview with Kenneth Tynan, quoted in Esslin, *The Theatre of the Absurd*, p. 290. In *Landscape* and *Silence* they are even more alone, we suspect, than when Pinter first made this comment in 1960.

77 Music and lyrics by Alan Jay Lerner. Popular songs do, of course, play a prominent part in the battle for positions between Anna and Deeley in *Old Times*.

78 Comparisons are made in, for instance, Gale, op. cit., p. 128; and Esslin, *Pinter: A Study of his Plays*, p. 126. (Esslin in fact claims that there is a difference in that 'in Pirandello's play either one, two or all three of the characters involved may be mad and therefore unable to realize the true situation'.)

79 'A Conversation (Pause) with Harold Pinter', p. 43.

80 Harold Hobson, *Sunday Times* (London), 25 May 1958.

81 In 'A Conversation (Pause) with Harold Pinter', p. 132.

82 Ibid., p. 133.

83 In Beckett too. When Estragon is asked what he did earlier in the evening, he replies 'I'm not a historian': *Waiting for Godot* (London, 1975), p. 65.

84 In reply to Gussow's question 'You're always the sum of your previous parts?', Pinter says 'But those previous parts are alive and present': 'A Conversation (Pause) with Harold Pinter', p. 133.

85 Henri Bergson, *Introduction à la métaphysique* (January 1903; usually rendered as *The Creative Mind*), ch. 4 (our translation).

86 On the cinematic quality of Anna's entrance, see Steven H. Gale, 'The Use of a Cinematic Device in Harold Pinter's *Old Times*', *Notes on Contemporary Literature* (1980).

87 We refer, of course, to the opening lines of Eliot's 'Burnt Norton', from *Four Quartets*. Gale, in *Butter's Going Up*, p. 188, suggests that *Old Times* is in fact a 'dramatization of these lines'.

88 *Old Times* is reminiscent in this sense of *La Manivelle*, a play by Robert Pinget with which Pinter may well have been acquainted through Beckett's translation in 1960 (which had the similar title *The Old Tune*). Here two old men reminisce over past events, never managing to agree on a solitary point, since, like Anna and Deeley, they both choose to remember a very different past.

89 As paraphrased in Thomas P. Adler, 'From Flux to Fixity: Art and Death in Pinter's *No Man's Land*', *Arizona Quarterly* (1979), p. 198.

90 'A Conversation (Pause) with Harold Pinter', p. 43.

91 Dukore, op. cit., p. 106.

92 See John Lahr, 'Pinter the Spaceman', in Lahr (eds), op. cit., pp. 175–93.

93 See Albert E. Kalson, 'The Artist as Con Man in *No Man's Land*', *Modern Drama*, 23 (1980), pp. 339–49.

94 'A Conversation (Pause) with Harold Pinter', p. 135.

95 It is often presumed that Pinter alone was responsible for the eventual 'solution' of the double-time problem posed by the novel. In fact, Pinter himself suggested that it was Karel Reisz's idea in an open seminar at the University of East Anglia, 1981.

96 Oliver Sacks, *Awakenings* (London, 1973).

97 In 'Harold Pinter Replies', interview with Harry Thompson, *New Theatre Magazine* (January 1961), p. 9.

BIBLIOGRAPHY

WORKS BY HAROLD PINTER

Plays

Plays: One. (*The Birthday Party, The Room, The Dumb Waiter, A Slight Ache, A Night Out.*) Master Playwrights. London: Eyre Methuen, 1976. New York: Grove Press, 1977.

Plays: Two. (*The Caretaker, The Collection, The Lover, Night School, The Dwarfs.*) Master Playwrights. London: Eyre Methuen, 1977. New York: Grove Press, 1977.

Plays: Three. (*The Homecoming, Tea Party, The Basement, Landscape, Silence.*) Master Playwrights. London: Eyre Methuen, 1978. New York: Grove Press, 1978.

Plays: Four. (*Old Times, No Man's Land, Betrayal, Monologue, Family Voices.*) Master Playwrights. London: Eyre Methuen, 1981. New York: Grove Press, 1981.

The Hothouse. London: Eyre Methuen, 1980. New York: Grove Press, 1980.

Other Places: Three Plays. (*Family Voices, A Kind of Alaska, Victoria Station.*) London: Methuen London, 1982.

Screenplays

Five Screenplays. (*The Servant, The Pumpkin Eater, The Quiller Memorandum, Accident, The Go-Between.*) London: Eyre Methuen, 1971. New York: Grove Press, 1973.

The Proust Screenplay. (*A la recherche du temps perdu.*) In collaboration with Joseph Losey and Barbara Bray. London: Eyre Methuen, 1977. New York: Grove Press, 1977.

The Screenplay of The French Lieutenant's Woman. With a foreword by John Fowles. London: Cape in association with Eyre Methuen, 1981. Boston, Mass.: Little, Brown, 1981.

The French Lieutenant's Woman and other Screenplays. (*The French Lieutenant's Woman, The Last Tycoon, Langrishe Go Down.*) London: Methuen London, 1982.

Non-dramatic work

Poems and Prose 1949–1977. London: Eyre Methuen, 1978. New York: Grove Press, 1978.

Selected interviews

'An Interview with Lawrence M. Bensky'. Repr. in C. Marowitz and S. Trussler (eds), *Theatre at Work*. London: Eyre Methuen, 1967.

'A Conversation (Pause) with Harold Pinter'. Interview with Mel Gussow. *New York Times Magazine*, 5 December 1971, pp. 42–3, 126–36.

'An Open Seminar at UEA'. Group discussion at the University of East Anglia, Norwich, led by C. W. E. Bigsby, October 1981. Text not yet available.

SELECTED BIBLIOGRAPHY

Gale, Steven H. *Harold Pinter: An Annotated Bibliography*. Boston, Mass.: G. K. Hall, 1978.

Imhof, Rudiger. *Pinter: A Bibliography*. London: T.Q. Publications, 1975.

SELECTED CRITICISM OF HAROLD PINTER

Books

Dukore, Bernard F. *Harold Pinter*. Master Dramatists. London and Basingstoke: Macmillan, 1982.

Esslin, Martin. *Pinter: A Study of his Plays*. Rev. edn of *The Peopled Wound: The Plays of Harold Pinter*. London: Eyre Methuen, 1973.

Gabbard, Lucina Paquet. *The Dream Structure of Pinter's Plays: A Psychoanalytic Approach*. Madison, NJ: Associated University Presses, 1976.

Gale, Steven H. *Butter's Going Up: A Critical Analysis of Harold Pinter's Work*. Durham, NC: Duke University Press, 1977.

Ganz, Arthur (ed.). *Pinter: A Collection of Critical Essays*. Englewood Cliffs, NJ: Prentice-Hall, 1972.

Gordon, Lois G. *Stratagems to Uncover Nakedness: The Dramas of Harold Pinter*. Columbia, Mo.: University of Missouri Press, 1968.

Hollis, James R. *Harold Pinter: The Poetics of Silence*. Crosscurrents/ Modern Critiques. Carbondale, Ill.: Southern Illinois University Press, 1970.

Lahr, John and Anthea (eds). *A Casebook on Harold Pinter's The Homecoming*. New York: Grove Press, 1971.

Quigley, Austin E. *The Pinter Problem*. Princeton, NJ: University of Princeton Press, 1975.

Taylor, John Russell. *Harold Pinter*. London: Longmans Green, 1969.

Articles

Alexander, Nigel. 'Past, Present and Pinter'. *Essays and Studies*, 27 (1974), pp. 1–17.

Almansi, Guido. 'Harold Pinter's Idiom of Lies'. *Contemporary English Drama*, Stratford-upon-Avon Studies 19 (1981), pp. 78–92.

Anderson, Michael. 'Harold Pinter: Journey to the Interior'. In *Anger and Detachment: A Study of Arden, Osborne and Pinter*, pp. 88–115. London: Pitman, 1976.

Bernhard, F. J. 'Beyond Realism: The Plays of Harold Pinter'. *Modern Drama*, 8 (September 1965), pp. 185–91.

Brown, John Russell. 'Mr Pinter's Shakespeare'. *Critical Quarterly*, 5 (Autumn 1963), pp. 251–65.

—— 'Dialogue in Pinter and Others'. *Critical Quarterly*, 7 (Autumn 1965), pp. 225–43.

—— 'Harold Pinter: *The Birthday Party* and Other Plays', 'Harold Pinter: Gestures, Spectacle and Performance: *The Caretaker, The Dwarfs* and Other Plays', 'Harold Pinter: Action and Control: *The Homecoming* and Other Plays'. In *Theatre Language: A Study of Arden, Osborne, Pinter and Wesker*, pp. 15–117. London: Allen Lane, 1972.

Coe, Richard M. 'Logic, Paradox, and Pinter's *Homecoming*'. *Educational Theatre Journal*, 27 (1975), pp. 488–97.

Cohn, Ruby. 'The Absurdly Absurd: Avatars of Godot'. *Comparative Literature Studies*, 2 (1965), pp. 233–40.

Dennis, Nigel. 'Pintermania'. *The New York Review of Books*, 17 December 1970, pp. 21–2.

Esslin, Martin. 'Godot and his Children: Theater of Samuel Beckett and Harold Pinter'. *Experimental Drama*, 14 (1963), pp. 128–46.

—— 'Parallels and Proselytes: Harold Pinter'. In *The Theatre of the Absurd*, pp. 265–92. Rev. and enlarged edn. Harmondsworth: Penguin, 1968.

—— 'Pinter Translated'. *Encounter*, 30, 3 (March 1968), pp. 45–7.

Kennedy, Andrew E. K. 'Harold Pinter'. In *Six Dramatists in Search of a Language: Shaw, Eliot, Beckett, Pinter, Osborne, Arden*, pp. 165–91. Cambridge: Cambridge University Press, 1974.

Salmon, Eric. 'Harold Pinter's Ear'. *Modern Drama*, 17 (1974), pp. 363–75.

Taylor, John Russell. 'A Room and Some Views: Harold Pinter'. In *Anger and After: A Guide to the New British Drama*, pp. 321–61. Rev. edn. London: Methuen, 1969.